TEACHING AT KEY STAGE 1

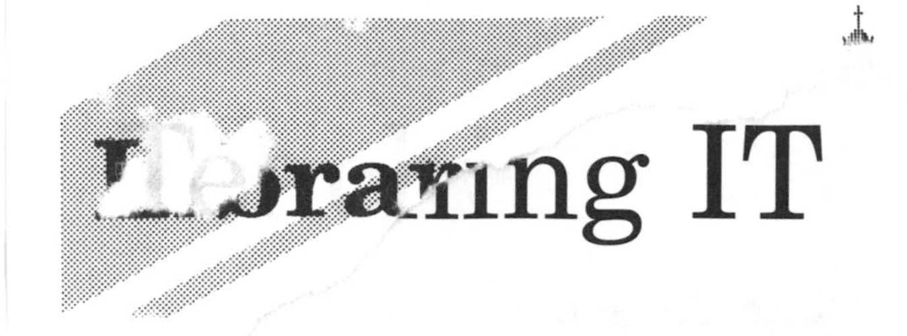

TEACHING AT KEY STAGE 1

Edited by Ann Sharp and Wendy Dewhirst

Teaching Topic Work Clare Benson

Teaching IT Richard Bennett

TEACHING AT KEY STAGE 1

Teaching IT

Richard Bennett

Acknowledgements

The author would like to thank the following, without whose help this book would not have been possible:

The teachers and children of:

Kelsall County Primary School, Cheshire
All Saints' CE Controlled Infant School, Chester
Kingsley County Primary School, Cheshire
Daresbury County Primary School, Cheshire
St James CE Controlled Primary School, Chester
Oldfield County Primary School, Chester

And with special thanks to:

Barbara Rigg of J.H. Godwin Primary School, Chester
Chris Holroyd of Werneth Infant School, Oldham
Jan Docker of Loughborough Infants School, Brixton
Jane Osmond of NCET
Linda Herrick of Huxley CE Primary School, Cheshire
Liz Brunooge of Gainsborough Infants School, Crewe
Maria Tarn of Cheshire Micro Centre
Marion Fraser of Sandiway County Primary School, Cheshire
Pauline Oultram of Moulton County Primary School, Cheshire
Rebecca Loades of Internet for Learning, RM plc
Steve Averill of Parkfield School, Birmingham

and all teachers, students and children in classrooms visited throughout the country who have directly or indirectly influenced the content of this book.

First published in 1997 by
Nash Pollock Publishing
32 Warwick Street
Oxford OX4 1SX

9 8 7 6 5 4 3 2 1

Orders to:
9 Carlton Close
Grove
Wantage
Oxfordshire OX12 0PU

A catalogue record ot this book is available from the British Library.

ISBN 1 898255 18 0

Typeset in 10.5/13pt New Century Schoolbook by Black Dog Design, Buckingham

Printed in Great Britain by Redwood Books, Trowbridge

Contents

Editors' preface

This is a series of books for teachers and student teachers to consolidate and extend their professional expertise across the curriculum and within the National Curriculum and RE. The series deals with the practical teaching issues and is focused on children at Key Stage 1 and under fives in reception classes.

A major theme through the books is that the voice of the child in the learning process must be heard. As teachers, we need to ensure that for the child the learning choices and experiences presented are relevant, purposeful and matched to the child's stage of development.

The young children involved at this key stage of their education will range from 4 to 7 years of age and represent, we believe, the best kind of learners. They will have begun to develop their own views, their own ways of making sense of new ideas, the world and their relationships; and should have an active and enthusiastic approach to life.

Of course, we also recognise that active young learners need sensitive control. Planned learning experiences with supportive and appreciative adults in their school world are a must.

There is no mystique about planning for and organising effective teaching and learning. The content of the National Curriculum is set out clearly in terms of knowledge, skills, concepts and attitudes. In this series, however, we are concerned to illustrate how a teacher can plan and organise the teaching of the Key Stage 1 curriculum using the developmental insights known about how young learners learn best.

We know that children learn best when actively engaged in the learning process and that an appropriate curriculum is integrated and relevant to the cultural needs of all children. First hand experiences matched with a child's stage of development are crucial for the young learner if sense is to be made of the demands of the various subject areas in Key Stage 1.

We know children bring and use diverse strategies and techniques for making sense of the learning process. As teachers, therefore we need to recognise that our teaching strategies and techniques have also to be varied and adaptable to match the learning needs of the children we teach and to give all children equal access to the whole curriculum.

Education is concerned with helping children become self-disciplined and self regulating, respecting the needs and rights of others. It must give children the necessary skills of knowledge, understanding and appreciation. The skills of numeracy, literacy and information technology are important in that they provide the child with access to such a knowledge and understanding. Education is also concerned with helping individuals to achieve personal fulfilment and to realise their own potential for living and working within their community and country.

Early childhood educational experiences begin this process. It is very important that learning is a stable, consistent and enjoyable experience. If learning is enjoyed it makes the world more interesting and comprehensible. It is likely to be sustained even when the learning requires perseverance, practice and efforts to learn tedious but necessary skills.

None of the areas of development must be neglected: the social, emotional physical and intellectual. To stress any one or two areas at the expense of the others leads to an incomplete person.

In planning the environment for teaching and learning we need to remember all these points and provide an environment and curriculum which will help the child grow in a positive way. The curriculum needs to be a balance between a child-centred and content-centred curriculum if all children are to receive their entitlement from the educational process.

The expert practitioners invited to write this series have had successful teaching careers. They are very aware of the need to link the theory with the practical curriculum. The suggestions and ideas give achievable and realistic outcomes for both the teacher and the child.

Guidance is given to enable the new teacher to become self-managing within the classroom and to help instill this same attribute in the children through the approach to the management and organisation of the classroom. The books have similar themes running through them: the management of children, the classroom, the curriculum, equal opportunities, assessment and recording, cross-curricular issues, resources and inspection.

Each book looks at what actually goes on in the classroom and how supportive and interested adults can enter into the learning partnership with the child. The importance of the school and its community having a close working partnership is also underlined, showing the necessity for children to feel a sense of worth and competence at school and in their home community.

The subjects of the National Curriculum are addressed separately but the authors understand that for the children at Key Stage 1 the curriculum is integrated and needs to be presented with that backdrop in mind. The purpose and context in which the subject specifics are taught are highly important if the learning is to be challenging and successful.

We hope that this series will encourage teachers in their teaching of Key Stage 1 and ensure that the curriculum continues to tap into and take advantage of the children's natural abilities and enthusiasms for learning ... and a teacher's enthusiasm for teaching.

Wendy Dewhirst
Ann Sharp

1 What this book is about

IT in a Key Stage 1 classroom

As you enter the classroom, you are immediately impressed by the atmosphere of calm efficiency. In one corner, a group of children is carefully mixing paint and applying it to pictures on easels. In the centre of the room, the teacher is working with a group on a reading and writing activity. In a nearby corner, a bay has been made from an arrangement of pieces of furniture. In this bay, two children are sitting at a computer keyboard discussing some writing on the monitor screen. One of them directs the pointer on the screen to a symbol, clicks a button and an array of small icons is shown on screen. The children spend a moment in discussion before moving the pointer over one of the icons and, with the another click of a button, a coloured picture of a dragon appears. The children giggle as they move it around the screen until it is positioned below the text. They go on to select another picture, of a tree, and place this beside the dragon. At this point, the teacher comes and peers over their shoulders, points at the screen and asks, "Was the dragon hiding behind the tree?"

The children re-read their writing on the screen and discuss the teacher's idea.

"Yeh, the dragon could jump out and frighten them [the children in the story]."

"But it's a friendly dragon."

"Yeh, but they don't know that."

"They could be frightened and then the dragon tells them not to and he's sad because no one wants to be his friend and they ..."

Figure 1.1 The children's completed story page

"Yeh, they say they will be his friend."

"Yeh!"

The teacher tells them this is a wonderful idea and after a little more discussion the children start adding more text.

Later that day, you find the children gathered on the floor around the teacher, who is reading from a book on her knee. From time to time, she turns the book around to show the children the pictures. You recognise the final page as that which the two children at the computer were creating earlier in the day. The story of the dragon and the village is not yet completed so the children discuss what might happen next. The following day you find two more children seated at the computer writing the next instalment of the story.

Collaborative story writing is not new to the infant classroom nor, these days, is the computer. Many children enter school having already developed some skills with, and awareness of, how computers operate. The children in the infant classroom described above will become adults in eleven or twelve years' time and, with Information Technology (IT) or the now so-called Information and Communication Technology changing so rapidly, it is almost impossible to speculate what computers will be capable of doing when they leave school.

And yet, we have to prepare today's children for tomorrow's world.

Teachers of infant-aged children play a significant part in providing children with core skills and knowledge – the building blocks of their future education – but they are also educating each child as an individual, at a particular and significant developmental stage in his/her life.

This book aims to show how young children can come to appreciate the value of computers and to provide suggestions for the teacher on how IT can contribute to children's learning.

Children and the classroom computer

The children at the computer in our typical infant classroom are not only developing skills in using the computer, they are learning about the use of a computer as a tool to help them achieve an objective – producing an illustrated story. They are also developing their skills in the use of language and gaining some appreciation of the significance of design to meet the needs of a particular and discerning audience – their peers.

It has been suggested (e.g. by Crook, quoted in Boyd Barrett & Scanlon, 1990) that while children are often grouped together in the infant classroom, they may not always be provided with opportunities to work collaboratively or co-operatively. When working at the computer, however, it has been shown (e.g. by Hill and Browne, 1988) that children as young as 5 engage in highly demanding negotiated decision-making tasks requiring the use of complex conversational skills and deep-level thinking, such as taking account of the views of others before carrying out an action.

Computers in a classroom can be used by children to:

- act as a catalyst or medium for the development of higher order thinking and language skills;
- provide low-level reinforcement of particular skills and knowledge in other areas of the curriculum;
- develop skills in and knowledge of the use of computers; and
- increase awareness of the role of the computer in assisting with the solution of problems in everyday life.

The teacher and the classroom computer

After helping the children with their desktop published story, their teacher makes a quick note in her class book about the two children's progress. At the end of the day she takes her laptop computer from her bag and transfers the notes she has made during the day to a database she keeps of the children's progress. She then reviews the progress of one child who is causing her concern. She scans a list of documents on the computer screen and "opens" one. An illustrated worksheet appears on the screen. She reads through it and makes a few minor amendments before connecting the printer and printing out a personalised worksheet for the child. She repeats this for three other worksheets, shuts the computer down and goes off to the staffroom to photocopy some sheets for groups of children.

It is not only the children who are developing IT capability. Increasingly, teachers are recognising the benefits which computers have for easing their workload and making administrative tasks such as record-keeping easier. The National Curriculum and the inspection process have intensified the need for teachers to keep accurate and detailed information about each child's progress. Changes in the requirements for the integration of children with special educational needs have placed greater responsibility on individual teachers and special needs co-ordinators in tracking children and arranging individualised teaching programmes. The amount of information which accumulates about each child, assessment processes, and the coverage of the curriculum seems to increase with each new term.

It has been shown that teachers who are themselves users of IT feel more confident and are more effective as teachers of IT (see Stager, 1995; NCET, 1994). A teacher who uses a computer to assist in her own work sees IT as a tool, a means to an end rather than an end in itself. The more IT is absorbed into the curriculum and integrated with existing activities, the easier and more naturally children develop their own confidence and competences.

Computers in a classroom can be used by the teacher to:

- record children's progress and help with the forward planning of a year group's, a class's, a class-group's and/or individual children's work programmes;
- assist in the production of individualised, high-quality teaching and learning materials;
- act as a role model in helping children come to appreciate the place of the computer in the everyday world, seeing IT as a useful tool and developing positive attitudes towards the application of IT to tasks.

This book aims to show how each of the objectives outlined in the two sections above can be achieved successfully in the primary school classroom, through the use of illustrative examples and practical advice.

IT and the National Curriculum

Since the introduction of the National Curriculum in England and Wales in 1988, IT has featured significantly at all stages. The Dearing Review of the whole curriculum in 1995 removed IT from within the Technology curriculum and raised its status to that of a core skill, legislating that IT should feature in a school's and all teachers' planning for every curriculum subject, apart from PE.

The revised document for IT provides a clear and unequivocal statement of the principal purpose of the IT curriculum; to develop pupils' information technology capability, which is characterised as: "an ability to effectively use IT tools and information sources to analyse, process and present information and to model, measure and control external events. This involves:

- using information sources and IT tools to solve problems
- using IT tools and information sources, such as computer systems and software packages, to support learning in a variety of contexts;
- understanding the implications of IT for working life and society".

(DFE &WO, 1995)

Returning to our initial example, the children writing the story were making use of an IT tool to present information and, by accessing pictures already stored in the computer, were using an information source to solve a problem. The computer was supporting the children's language learning and was providing them with an appreciation of the way in which IT is used by authors and illustrators to make the process of publishing easier.

In later chapters, we shall see how IT is used in a range of contexts, not only to develop an appreciation of the role of IT, but to support children's learning and to assist with the solution of problems.

What exactly is IT?

The National Curriculum statement about IT capability refers to "IT tools and information sources, such as computer systems and software packages", implying there may be more to IT than computers. The Curriculum Council for Wales suggests:

> Broadly speaking information technology could be taken to refer to any artefact or system which enhances the ability of humans to obtain and handle all sorts of information and to communicate information and ideas. Paper, pens and printing presses are all in this category, as are library systems. In more contemporary usage 'information technology' refers to electronic means of handling information. (CCW, 1990, para. A 1.2)

Consider the range of electronic equipment presently available which handles information: telephones, fax machines, televisions, video recorders, audio recorders, CD players, CD ROM devices, personal organisers, bar-code readers, radios, mobile phones, not to mention the Internet.

Although some mention is made to the use of video, audio tape recording, telephone and fax, this book focuses principally on the use of computers. It should be borne in mind, however, that the National Curriculum Orders are careful to keep the definition of IT broad. Children have an entitlement to make use of not only computers and software, but other forms of information technology during all phases of their schooling.

Whom is this book for?

This book is intended to be used by teachers and those training to become teachers of children from 4 to 7 years of age. The suggestions and examples contained in this book are drawn from direct classroom practice – often carried out by teachers and students with little background knowledge or confidence in the use of IT.

Very few primary teachers are trained IT experts, but the great virtue of the computer is that it allows one to experiment and learn through trial and improvement. The underlying message of this book is that the most effective way for children to learn how to use computers is through direct hands-on experience. The same is no less true for the teacher. It is assumed that the readers have a willingness and desire to find out more and will take the ideas presented in this book, adapt them and apply them to their own teaching and learning situations. With this in mind, a range of case studies, exemplars, ideas, suggestions and tips are provided. These are drawn from actual examples of classroom teaching, either experienced first hand or observed. All classrooms and teachers are different – what works for one teacher with one group of children may not work with another. It is hoped that the opportunity this book provides to metaphorically "peer over colleagues' shoulders" – even if only to say "Well, I wouldn't have done it like that!" – will help inform teachers' own practice.

What is the purpose of this book?

This book aims to be a practical reference guide, something which can be read from cover to cover, or can be dipped into for ideas. Where possible, it is shown how IT skills and knowledge can be developed within and alongside other aspects of the curriculum. Rather than IT being seen as something which needs to be added to a school's curriculum, the intention is to suggest, indicate and demonstrate ways in which IT can be used to help support, enhance and extend learning across all curriculum areas.

What is the focus of this book?

The teaching and learning principle which underlies this book is that the classroom situation can be represented by this diagram:

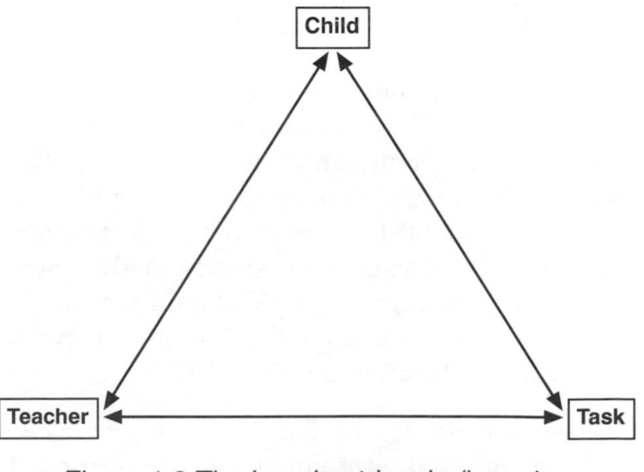

Figure 1.2 The learning triangle (based on Holloway, 1979)

The ideal learning environment is one in which the task and teacher's input are appropriately matched to the needs of the child. In some circumstances, the teacher's role may be the most significant – such as when a child and teacher are working closely together. At other times, the task may be the most important aspect, with the teacher's role being diminished – such as when a child is completing a piece of work unaided; finishing a drawing, for example. In all learning situations, the teacher will have had to ensure that the task or her interventions are matched to the skills, level of understanding and needs of the learner. Keeping this triangular relationship in equilibrium to meet the needs of the learner is the ultimate responsibility of the teacher. Which is where IT comes in. IT can be used to augment the role of the teacher or, more controversially, can assume some of the teacher's responsibilities. Conversely, a computer-based activity can be a task in its own right, or IT can be used to support, enhance or extend non-computer centred activities. A computer is capable of offering far more assistance and opening up far more opportunities than any other teaching and learning resource. Its usefulness is entirely dependent on the skills, awareness, confidence and imagination of the teacher. Hopefully, this book will raise awareness of what is possible and thereby increase the reader's confidence and willingness to have a go.

Summary

To reiterate the focus of this chapter, the classroom computer should be regarded as a tool to be used by the teacher to complement her work, either through direct use with children or indirectly to assist with her recording of children's progress or in the production of targeted learning support materials.

This book aims to provide information and guidance on how this can be achieved. Although it can be read through, from cover to cover, it is most likely that teachers will prefer to dip into chapters and sections, and so each section has been written with this in mind. Where cross-referencing is necessary, this is mentioned in the text.

References

Boyd Barrett, O. & Scanlon, E. (eds) (1990) *Computers and Learning*; Addison Wesley

CCW (1990) *IT in the National Curriculum: Non-statutory Guidance*; Curriculum Council for Wales

DFE & WO (1995) *Information Technology in the National Curriculum*; HMSO

Hill, A. & Browne, A. (1988) Talk and the Microcomputer: An Investigation in the Infant Classroom; *Reading*, vol. 22 (1), pp. 61–9

Holloway, C. (1979) *Cognitive Psychology: Block 4: Learning and Problem Solving (part 1): Learning and Instruction*; Open University Press

NCET (1994) *Portable Computers Pilot Evaluation: Full report*; National Council for Educational Technology

Stager, S. S. (1995) Constructing Staff Development and Educational Change; in Tinsley, J. D. & van Weert, T. J. (eds) *Liberating the Learner: Proceedings of the Sixth International Federation for Information Processing World Conference on Computers in Education, 1995*; Chapman & Hall

2 The IT curriculum

What this chapter is about

This chapter examines the curriculum for IT, within and beyond the National Curriculum requirements. It addresses the following questions:

- What exactly should children be learning in IT at Key Stage 1?
- How could IT skills, knowledge and understanding be planned to ensure progression through and beyond Key Stage 1?
- What resources might be needed for IT at Key Stage 1?

Delivering the IT curriculum

The National Curriculum documentation for IT stresses the importance of using IT as a tool, making use of IT to solve problems, investigating and manipulating information sources, enhancing learning in other areas of the curriculum. IT education, it is implied, should be seen as a means to an end and not an end in itself. The documentation also emphasises the need for children to learn about IT itself; to develop skills and knowledge in the application of IT and an understanding of how IT is used in the world at large.

In Chapter 3, we shall see how the use of computers can have an impact upon the way in which children learn. Unlike most other teaching and learning aids, computers are interactive – they can be made to respond to the actions of the user. Although computers can be used to support existing classroom activities, they can, if used wisely, enhance and extend learning opportunities made available for children.

At Key Stage 1, children should be provided with opportunities to use IT to:

- communicate information,
- handle information,
- model real and imaginary situations, and
- control events.

In most cases, this should be done in the context of work in other areas of the curriculum by making use of IT as a tool. But what do these strands mean in practice? How should they be taught?

Communicating information

What follows is an overview of the communicating strand of the IT curriculum. Each of the activities mentioned is fleshed out in more detail in later sections of this book, principally Chapters 4 and 5.

Word processing and the editing and drafting process

In the previous chapter we saw how a class of 6- and 7-year-olds used the computer to write an ongoing class story. Not only were the children developing skills in using a computer, they were gaining an appreciation of the versatility of word processing. Once pages were produced, they could later be modified to make the story more coherent. We can all probably remember being told, at some time in our own schooling, "That's lovely, dear, could you write a bit more?" Our recourse was often to add more text to the end of our work as this was the only place where there was space. However, this was often not the place where more writing was needed, particularly if our account of the trip to the zoo already concluded with "And then I went home for tea".

A word processor allows text to be inserted, edited, moved or deleted anywhere in a document. For this reason, it is an extremely valuable tool, not only for developing children's editing and redrafting but for encouraging children to "work-up" or improve a piece of written work. This has important implications for the development of children's thinking and planning skills.

For their topic about books, a group of 5-year-olds wrote letters to their favourite authors. To make the task easier, they jointly word processed a general letter, which was then personalised for each author.

Tarporley County Primary School

Headteacher: Mr. R. Coates

Park Road
Tarporley
Cheshire
CW6 0AN
Today's date

Author's name
c/o Author's publisher
Publisher's address

Dear Author's name

We hope you are well.

We are in a class of six and seven year olds and our school is having a Book Week on July 5th. In our class we voted for our favourite books. A lot of the children liked name of author's book. Can you tell us how you thought of the story? We find thinking up stories quite hard and would like some tips.

We wrote this letter on our word processor. We like using the computer. Do you use a word processor?

We hope you will be writing some more books soon.

Yours sincerely

Your names
(on behalf of Class 9)

Figure 2.1 A 'personalised' word processed letter to authors

The children's letters and the replies were proudly mounted in a class book specially made, bound and displayed during the school's Book Week.

Letter writing is an obvious and purposeful way of encouraging children to consider the needs of the audience when communicating information. The activity described above could have been carried out with pencil and paper but the added value of using a computer was increased flexibility and the groundwork this activity laid for developing the children's understanding of the role of computerised systems in producing personalised mail.

Pictures and graphics

Painting pictures on the computer is fast becoming the most common use of the computer since the introduction of computers with mouse control. A child's picture can be copied from a graphics program or a file of clip-art pictures and simply "pasted" into place in a piece of writing. Most word processing software can these days incorporate pictures within text. Pictures (including photos) can often be copied from CD ROM packages such as encyclopaedias and pasted into a children's piece of written work. Children can have their own photos imported into a computer either through use of a digital camera, by processing a film into a photo CD or by the use of a scanner. With a little practice, a clip-art picture can be taken into a graphics program and modified before being used to illustrate a piece of writing. (See Chapter 5 – "Geography, History and IT".)

Desktop publishing

The children described in the introduction were using a simple desktop publishing (DTP) package called *Fairy Tales* (Resource), running on a BBC B computer. Text is combined with pictures made from a library of picture elements which are positioned (pasted) by the children on the screen.

Figure 2.2 A desktop published page from a book written by 5- and 6-year olds

Desktop publishing refers to the manipulation of text and graphic images on the computer screen, the results of which are then printed out. Some programs are specifically designed for use by Key Stage 1 children and have simplified methods for selecting and positioning pictures on the screen.

Music and sound

Music programs abound, owing to the computer's capabilities in synthesising sound and the ease with which music can be processed, in much the same way as text can be edited. Children can manipulate sound to compose music, "record" their own sounds and voices into the computer to narrate stories, practise their reading, or put sound effects into multimedia presentations.

Multimedia

Multimedia presentations combine text, pictures, sound, music and even moving images. Most CD ROM packages make extensive use of multimedia.

Progression in communicating information

The National Curriculum requirements are left deliberately vague to encourage schools to define their own schemes of work based on the skeletal framework of the statutory statements. Table 2.1 provides a suggested line of progression of skill development in communicating information in IT.

Stage 1	Creating a scene by pasting picture elements from a library of images (e.g. *My World*) Creating simple sentences using words selected from concept keyboard overlays
Stage 2	Creating scenes related to particular subject or topic, using bank of images Completing or writing short passages, or writing captions, poems or letters using a word bank created by the teacher Printing pictures and text
Stage 3	Simple desktop publishing using dedicated educational packages (e.g. *Fairy Tales*) More extended word processing – e.g. collaborative story writing Creating original graphics images (e.g. patterns with shape and colour) Composing original musical pieces using phrases (e.g. *Compose World*) Loading and saving files
Stage 4	Word processing – cutting, copying and pasting text Transferring text and/or graphics between files (e.g. using clip–art images to create a scene or incorporating clip–art pictures into a piece of text) Creating original pictures for a particular purpose (e.g. a Christmas card)
Stage 5	Simple multimedia stories or information presentations Formatting text – using paragraphs and indents Using zoom to edit their own or clip art images

Table 2.1 Progression in communicating information

Handling information

Simply by providing an opportunity for children to save, load and edit their own word processed documents (Stage 3), a teacher would be going some way to meeting the minimum requirements laid down in the National Curriculum for the handling of information. However, this would be denying children the opportunity to make use of the computer's powerful capabilities for handling data and information.

Databases

Databases come in a variety of forms. The most common is the "flat file", which is similar to a card index system, with each card being represented by a screen of information. Each screen or "record" contains information under headings. This information can be searched, selected, sorted and graphed.

When a class of 5- and 6-year-olds was studying the topic of "Ourselves", the children were interested in gathering statistical information about themselves and each other. They created a record card for each child on which were "fields" of information.

Once the data had been entered, the children were able to compare numerical data about themselves with figures for children in a class of 9- and 10-year-olds. The first thing they noticed was the difference in the distribution of hair colour of the children in the other class. There were more dark-haired children and fewer with fair or blond hair. The children wondered whether people's hair grew darker as they became older.

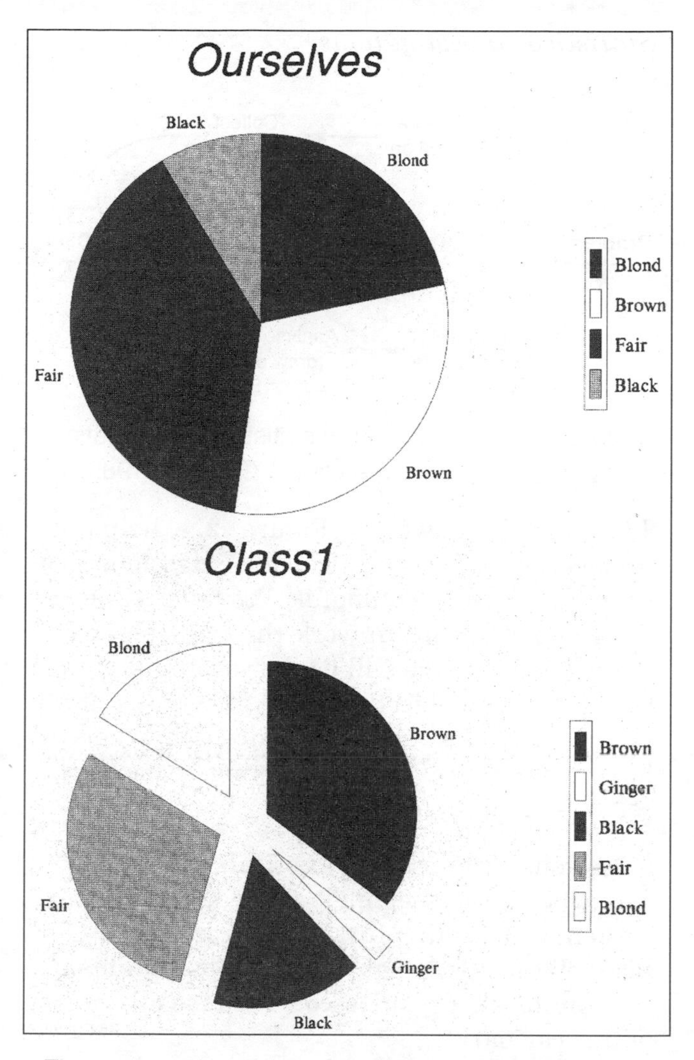

Figure 2.3 Pie charts of 6-year-olds' ("Ourselves") and 10-year-olds' ("Class 1") hair colours

Statistical information such as this can be gathered and analysed without a computer but the advantage of the computer lies in the flexibility and versatility with which the information can be manipulated. To make their comparisons, the children in the above example found pie charts were the most useful form of graphical representation (Figure 2.3).

Note how the two pie charts showing hair colour can be compared side by side. As can be seen, there is a greater proportion of dark-haired children (brown and black) in Class 1's chart. As the data are represented by circles of the same diameters, a direct comparison can be made, despite the fact there are 23 children shown in the "Ourselves" chart and 37 children in the "Class 1" chart.

Graphs are produced almost instantaneously once information has been entered into a database. Children (or the teacher) can keep drawing and interpreting graphs until some are found which provide them with information. Imagine how long it would take to draw ten different graphs with pencil and paper. More importantly, while 5-year-olds can readily interpret pie charts, most adults would have difficulty carrying out the necessary calculations with fractions and angles to draw one.

The great value in using a computer database for statistical work is that it places far more emphasis on the interpretation of data.

Statistical investigations

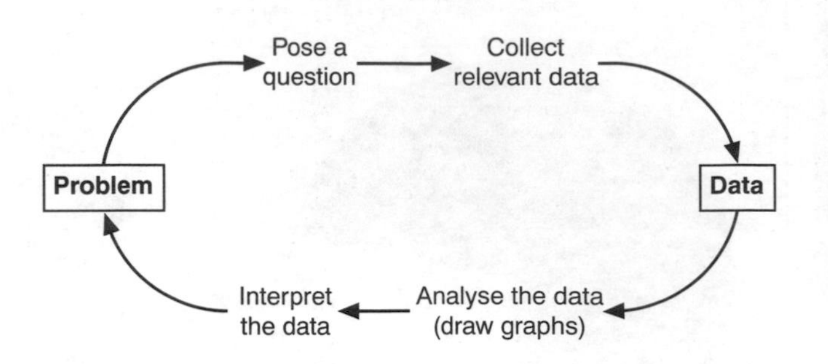

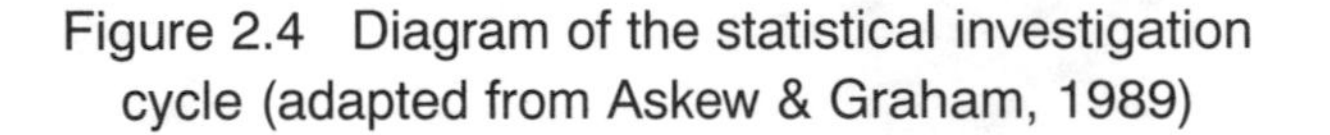
Figure 2.4 Diagram of the statistical investigation cycle (adapted from Askew & Graham, 1989)

The model shown in Figure 2.4 helps us understand how statistical investigations can be made more meaningful. Provided children have opportunities to work through the entire process, each stage will be purposefully related to the original objective – the answering of an interesting question. The children will thereby have a vested interest in making sense of the result – the graphs.

Questions requiring statistical investigation can arise out of seemingly everyday situations: "When you grow, your feet get bigger", "Our next class story ought to be about animals", "My mum shops at Tesco's because it's got a better car park".

The last statement was used by a group of 6-year-olds to investigate the shopping habits of their parents.

One disadvantage of a database is that the format for the records has to be created before the database can be used. In effect, the record "cards" which will hold the information need to be designed by either the teacher or the children.

Graph-drawing programs

If the drawing of graphs is all that is required, then there is a range of simple graph drawing packages available (e.g. *Graph IT!* (Sherston), *DataGraph* (Topologika)) which only require the data to be entered into a table or chart on screen. Another solution is to invest in a spreadsheet program.

Spreadsheets

A spreadsheet is in essence a very large sheet of squared paper in an electronic form. Each square, or cell, can hold information in the form of text or numbers. The great power of the spreadsheet lies in its capability for linking cells with mathematical formulae. This makes the spreadsheet a versatile tool for use in any situation in which information can be presented in the form of a table. There is no specific requirement for children at Key Stage 1 to make use of a spreadsheet but it can provide a quick and painless means of drawing graphs without having to create a database file.

Ready-made information files

In addition to creating their own information by gathering and interpreting their own data, children can have access to ready-made information stored on computer disk. Some schools keep database and spreadsheet files created by their children for use by later or younger classes. Another alternative is for a teacher or parent helper to create files for use by her children which can provide valuable hands-on experience for the teacher in the use of the software. A useful exercise for a school's Professional Development Day can be for the staff to get to grips with their data-handling software by working through the statistical investigations cycle and producing some data files for later use by children. (See Chapter 7 for further INSET ideas.)

CD ROM

Now many schools have access to at least one CD ROM drive, the range of information which can be accessed by children can be quite astounding. Although good CD ROM packages are expensive, they are very easy to use and highly accessible. Not only do they provide children with a highly motivating entry route into data handling, they are a requirement of the Geography National Curriculum. (See Chapter 5, "History, Geography and IT".)

The children devised a questionnaire which was taken home and completed by parents. The children held various views (hypotheses) as to what determined their parents' supermarket shopping preferences:

- "The food is better at Sainsbury's."
- "My mum likes a cup of coffee, so she goes to Tesco's."
- "We haven't got a car, so we go to the Spar shop."

Their views affected the type of questions which went into the questionnaire, as they were anxious to find out which were the most significant factors affecting adults' choice of supermarket.

The information from the questionnaires was entered into a simple database (OUR FACTS on a BBC computer) and a series of graphs was printed out to find the answers to the children's questions:

- Which supermarkets do our parents go to?
- How often do they visit the supermarket?
- Why do they go to that supermarket?

Their graphs held meaning for the children as they could be used to answer their initial questions.

Our shopping survey

Do you live in or around Blacon? ☒ Yes ☐ No

Which shop(s) are you going or have you been to?
☐ Newsagent ☐ Greengrocer
☐ Chip shop ☐ Video library
☐ Off licence ☒ Post Office
☐ Spar ☐ Chemist
☐ Happy Shopper ☐ Davies

Why do you like it (them)?
☐ Cheap ☒ Good service
☐ Sells everything ☐ Sell what I need
☐ Friendly ☐ Sells nice things
☐ Modern ☐ Plenty of choice
☐ Local

Which shop(s) do you like best?
☐ Newsagent
☐ Chip shop
☐ Off licence
☒ Spar
☐ Happy Shopper
☐ Greengrocer
☐ Video library
☐ Post Office
☐ Chemist
☐ Davies
☐ Butchers

Do we need other shops in Blacon? ☐ Yes ☒ No

Which do we need?
☐ Ornament shop
☐ A free shop
☐ A fishing tackle shop
☐ A flower shop
☐ A computer shop
☐ An electrical shop (Norweb)
☐ An ice cream shop
☐ a clothes shop
☐ A shoe shop
☐ A pet shop
☐ A joke and magic shop
☐ a DIY shop
☐ A music shop
☐ A book shop
☐ A cafe
☐ A sports shop
☐ A furniture shop
☐ A McDonalds

Do we need any of these:
☒ A swimming pool
☒ An animal hospital
☐ A small zoo
☐ A car rental showroom
☐ A theatre
☐ A hospital for poor people
☐ A police station
☐ An ambulance station
☐ A museum
☐ A butterfly farm

Is there anything else Blacon needs? ☐ Yes ☒ No

What?

Figure 2.5 A questionnaire on shopping habits, devised by 6-year olds

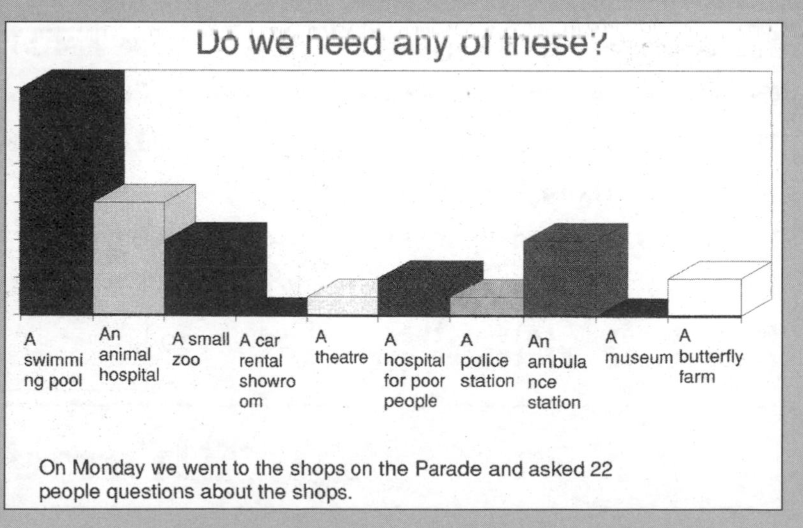

Figure 2.6 A graph produced from the shopping survey

When the teacher of a top infant class wanted to develop her children's skills with databases, she created a data file of very suspicious-sounding criminals.

She then wrote some crime stories for the children to solve. The children had to search through the file for the most likely suspects, using the partial descriptions contained in her "newspaper" reports. The children were so impressed with the idea, they went on to create their own villains and design their own data file and word processed crime stories.

Villains file

Name: Scrappy Sam
Hair colour: Brown
Eye colour: Blue
Lips: Bumpy
Age: Old
Height: Tall
Features: Scar on left cheek
Crimes: Murder and robbing

Artist's Impression

Figure 2.7 The record of one villain

CREWE TIMES 20P

12 APRIL 1996

ROBBER STEALS SOME MONEY

This morning Mrs Tomos woke up
There was a nose downstairs
Mrs tomos went downstairs
There was a rober
HE was stealing her mony
Mrs Tomos shouted HELP!!!
The rober ran away
Mrs tomas told the police a description of the rober

The rober was midle age
He had black hair and a berd
He had a scare on his nose
If you see this man tell the police
Call 999

by Shamed

Progression in handling information

Table 2.2 provides a suggested line of progression for the handling of information. It builds upon the minimum requirement expressed in the National Curriculum and should provide a sound basis for children's work in Key Stage 2.

Stage 1	Simple, practical data gathering and analysis (graphing) without the use of the computer (e.g. children's heights represented on the classroom wall)
Stage 2	Drawing and interpreting graphs from simple surveys suggested by the children. The data gathered by the children but entered for them in the database/graphing program by an adult
Stage 3	Simple question-led surveys, analysed with a graphing package or simple spreadsheet (class- or group-based) Searching for information on a simple CD ROM package (e.g. *My First Encyclopaedia* (Guildsoft))
Stage 4	Interrogating a data file created by the teacher (e.g. criminals) Entering additional data into the teacher's file
Stage 5	Designing and using a database file to investigate particular questions as a class/group (e.g. shopping survey)

Table 2.2 Progression in handling information

Modelling

What is modelling?

The National Curriculum requirement for modelling states: "Pupils should be taught to use IT based models or simulations to explore aspects of real or imaginary situations" (DFE, 1995).

Scientists, technologists and designers use computer modelling to test their ideas. A "model" of the Severn Bridge will have been extensively tested for strength with a computer before the bridge itself was constructed. In the Key Stage 1 classroom, children are unlikely to use the computer for such heavyweight tasks but it could enable them to become involved in an adventure to rescue imprisoned children, to explore a medieval castle, or to guide a real or imaginary robot around a maze. This is achieved through the use of adventure programs, computer simulations or simple programming applications such as *Tiny LOGO* (Topologika).

Adventure programs

There are many adventure programs written for young children which enable them to participate in decision making to determine the outcome of the story. Perhaps the best known is *Granny's Garden* (4mation), which was originally available for the BBC computer, but has now been released on CD ROM in a far more sophisticated form.

In *Granny's Garden*, the children are asked to assist in releasing children who have been captured by a witch. By responding to a series of situations presented in the form of text and pictures, the children have puzzles to solve and decisions to make at various key points in the story.

An adventure program such as *Granny's Garden* can be used in a number of ways:

- *The class adventure*. Just as the children gather together to hear a class story, they group together to explore the next stage in the adventure story. The puzzles are either solved there and then or form the basis for maths investigational work away from the computer. A classroom display of the children's progress through the program often accompanies this approach.
- *Group adventures*. When there is a wide spread of ability within a class, not all children will be participants in a class adventure. A group of children of similar ability could work together on an adventure periodically.

- *Pairs or small groups working independently*. Some teachers like the competitive edge this can provoke – others prefer to encourage co-operation and the sharing of ideas.

Computer simulations

Simulations of real events or situations are less common for Key Stage 1 classrooms, where first-hand experience is a far more powerful learning medium. Some of the more simple simulations provide opportunities for children to practise specific skills, such as the manipulation of money (e.g. *Supermarket* (Resource). Their advantage lies in the way the computer is able to monitor the children's responses and adjust the level of demand to suit the needs of the child. It is as yet uncertain as to the extent to which this type of experience is transferrable to real-life situations, and vice versa.

Progression in modelling

Unlike the communicating and handling of information, the skills required to make use of computer simulations and adventure programs are more related to the complexity of the software than the development of a program's use as a tool. Table 2.3 below suggests a progression which could be used to select software or the way it is used.

Stage 1	Exploring a simple adventure program or simulation Developing a systematic approach
Stage 2	Exploring a simple adventure program or simulation, explaining and justifying decisions taken Recording progress and discoveries using their own methods
Stage 3	Exploring an adventure program or simulation more systematically, recording and communicating progress Investigating associated problems with and away from the computer

Table 2.3 Progress in modelling with a computer

Control

What is control?

The underlying principle of control is that devices can be made to carry out predetermined actions. In its simplest form, control can apply to an electrical circuit which includes a switch – the switch can be said to control the light. More complex devices can be made to carry out a series of instructions, such as an automatic washing machine or a video recorder which has been "programmed" to record particular TV programmes. A computer program is essentially a list of instructions which commands a computer to carry out a set of actions. In the infant classroom, children are not expected to write computer programs, but they can be given opportunities to develop important foundation skills and knowledge which will enable them to subsequently approach programming and control tasks in a systematic and logical fashion.

Programmable robots or turtles

Many schools now have programmable robotic toys such the Roamer (Valiant) or Pip (Swallow) turtles. These versatile computerised vehicles can be programmed to travel around the floor in a predictable manner. The children enter a series of commands by pressing keys on the turtle's back which determine the distance it travels and the amount it turns.

Floor turtle programming provides an highly relevant and motivating introduction to LOGO computer programming. With LOGO, the children control the movements of a small turtle on the computer screen by typing in simple instructions such as FORWARD 10 LEFT 90.

LOGO programming

LOGO is an extremely versatile programming language which enables children to take control of the computer – rather than vice versa (see Chapter 4, "Mathematics and IT"). In addition, LOGO allows children to, among other things:

- draw pictures,

Fig 2.9 Children using a Roamer programmable turtle

Groups of 5-year-olds in one infant school were given an opportunity to use the Roamer turtle as part of their topic on "Journeys". A simple "road" was drawn on a large sheet of paper and the children were asked to take turns to type a new instruction into the Roamer. After each new instruction was added, the turtle was returned to the start and the "GO" button was pressed to see how well the turtle negotiated the route. An older, more able child was included in each group to make a written record of each entry so that if a mistake was made, the list of instructions could be erased and retyped. The teacher realised that after using the turtle, most children were able to differentiate left from right and several understood what was meant by a right angle (although Thomas insisted there should also be a left angle!). Although a self-professed sceptic of IT, the teacher felt sure the turtle was one of the most successful approaches she had come across for introducing the concept of angular measurement and body-centred geometry (i.e. left and right). The children had also been involved in logical, step-by-step problem solving.

- learn about shape and space,
- learn about numbers in a visual context,
- develop problem-solving skills,
- apply and develop higher level thinking and language skills,
- write and play music, and
- control devices.

There are now several versions of LOGO which are available for young children (e.g. *TINY LOGO* (Topoligika)) and some simple adventure programs (e.g. *Crystal Rainforest* (Sherston) or *The Playground* (Topologika)) which provide easy entry routes into LOGO programming by creating imaginary contexts for the control of devices.

Progression in control

Table 2.4 provides a suggested approach to the development of children's knowledge and skills in the use of IT for control purposes.

Stage 1	Practical work on body-centred directions (left and right) away from the computer (e.g. guiding a blind-folded child by giving verbal instructions)
Stage 2	Exploring the environment by programming a floor turtle
Stage 3	Programming a floor robot to negotiate a simple maze Working with adventure programs containing elements of LOGO programming (e.g. *The Playground* (Topologika))
Stage 4	Drawing on screen with a turtle graphics program (e.g. *Tiny LOGO* (Topologika))

Table 2.4 Progression in control

What sort of hardware might a school need for IT?

(Please refer to Appendix I for explanations of some of the computer terminology contained in this section.)

"Hardware" is defined as the physical equipment, such as the keyboard, computer, monitor, printer, disk drives, CD ROM drive, concept keyboard, and so on.

Computer systems can be confusing for the unitiated but there are sound educational reasons for investing in more modern, hard-disk-based computers with mouse control for use by young children.

- The "windows" screen display relies less on text and more on symbols.
- The use of a mouse for communicating with the computer places less reliance on the use of the keyboard.
- A hard disk drive makes the technicalities of loading and saving programs and files considerably easier for children and teachers.
- The software which runs on the newer machines is much more appealing and educationally sound than some of the early programs.
- Only the more recent computers can run CD ROM drives which offer a range of highly attractive and useful interactive software packages.

The suggested minimum hardware requirements for an infant school or department are therefore:

- at least one computer per classroom/ teaching area;
- each computer to have a disk drive and printer for use by children;
- at least one computer in the school/ department with a hard drive, capable of running a CD ROM drive system;
- at least one colour printer, compatible with all computers;
- concept keyboards (or similar) for use with at least half the computers.

At the earliest opportunity, however, the school should aim to provide all classrooms with more modern, hard-disk-based machines. More details of hardware are contained in Appendix II.

What sort of software should an infant school or department have?

"Software" refers to the programs or applications which are used on the computer. No "recommended" list of software can ever be definitive, owing to the rapid development of IT and the situational vagaries of each school and its needs. However, the following list of suggested areas to be addressed ought to provide a starting point for a school in checking its provision. A more detailed list of titles for each type of computer (BBC, Acorn, RM, PC, Apple) is contained in Appendix III.

Communicating information

- A simple word processor, with text editing (i.e. the ability to cut, copy and paste text). Many word processors have the added feature of a voice synthesiser which can read back a child's piece of text.
- A more powerful word processor or desktop publishing package which allows children to combine text with pictures
- A simple graphics program based on set shapes such as squares and circles
- Sets of clip-art files related to specific topics
- A more sophisticated graphics program with editing and zoom features
- A simple music-writing program

Handling information

- A simple database program for entering, searching and presenting information in graphs

- A more powerful database program which enables the teacher to control the features made available for the children and which allows for the comparison of sets of data
- A simple spreadsheet or graph-drawing program
- A suite of programs which includes compatible spreadsheet, database, word-processor and graphics programs (optional)
- Educational CD ROM based encyclopaedia packages

Modelling

- A general adventure program unrelated to a specific topic
- Adventure programs related to specific themes or topics (optional)
- Simulations related to specific topics on disk or CD ROM (optional)

Control

- At least one programmable turtle robot
- A simulation or adventure which requires children to sequence events (optional)
- An introductory version of LOGO
- A full version of LOGO (optional)

Other

- Software to support learning in specific areas of the curriculum (see Chapters 4 and 5)

Summary

In this chapter we have examined the National Curriculum requirements for IT, and explored ways of developing these further. Some indication has been given as to how each strand of IT (communicating and handling information, modelling and control) can be developed through the use of practical examples and suggested activities.

Some guidance has also been provided on the sorts of hardware and software which an infant school or department should consider making available for the development of children's IT capability.

References

Askew, M. & Graham, M. (1989) *Using Mathematical Thinking: Block 2: Investigating with Mathematics*; Unit 7: Solving Problems in the Classroom; Open University Press

DFE (1995) *Information Technology in the National Curriculum*; HMSO

3 The child and IT

What this chapter is about

When a child sits down in front of a computer, what should a teacher know about the relationship between the child and the computer? This chapter addresses some of the issues underlying this relationship, namely:

- What a child needs to learn about using IT
- How IT contributes to children's learning
- How IT could be used to meet the individual needs of children, including those with special educational needs
- What the educational effects and implications for working in groups around the computer are
- The extent to which teachers should be aware of gender and equal opportunities issues when organising IT work for children

IT and children's learning

When making use of a computer, children should not only be learning how to make use of IT, they need also to learn when and why IT might be useful. But there is more to IT than a body of knowledge and a set of skills to be acquired. We talk of a computer "user" rather than using a term that denotes passivity such as "viewer" or "audience". Unlike a book or a TV programme, a computer responds to the actions of the person using it. It is this interactive aspect which sets computer work apart from other areas of the curriculum. IT can be a tool, a slave, or a master, or can become a useful companion or guide. Having considered the learning triangle described in the first chapter, we can see that IT is able to take on the role of the teacher as well as the task. So where does the child fit into this relationship?

Who is in control?

IT capability centres around the development of children's confidence and competence to use computers (and other IT tools) independently and purposefully to solve problems and assist with their learning. In other words, children have control over the computer – telling it what they want it to do. However, computers have the capability to exert control over children's actions, hence the obsession some children have for computer games. Having some appreciation of the relationship between the child and the computer while engaged in educational activities is essential for any teacher wishing to develop children's IT capability. It is also important in being able to take advantage of the computer's role in a learning situation and use it for the teacher's own educational ends.

A useful model of the learning situation when working with a computer is represented by the diagram in Figure 3.1

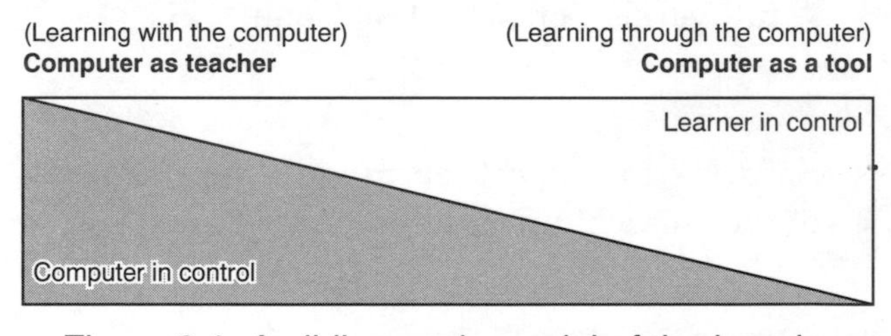

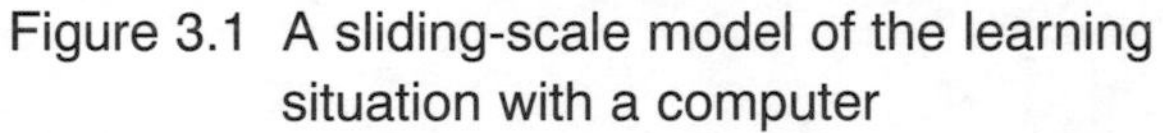
Figure 3.1 A sliding-scale model of the learning situation with a computer

Activities are placed on the scale somewhere between the left and right ends, depending on the level of control exerted by either the learner or the computer.

An activity placed at the left end of the scale implies the computer acts as an authoritarian teacher, instructing the child and controlling his actions. An activity placed at the right end of the scale suggest the child is in control of the computer and the learning situation – the child is using the computer as a tool.

In developing IT capability, a teacher's aim is to provide opportunities and develop skills which increasingly put the child in control of the computer – using IT as a tool to assist with his learning or to solve problems.

This computer-based learning gauge can help the teacher analyse the relationship between the learner and the computer. Plotting the position of an activity on the gauge provides an indication for the teacher as to the extent to which the child or the computer is in control. Shifting the emphasis of the activity more towards the right end of the gauge improves its potential for developing IT capability.

Joel and Bethan (4 and 5 years old) have been given a colour-and shape-matching activity to carry out on the computer. They have not been at the school very long and the teacher is providing them with some IT experience in a familiar, non-threatening context. The children are presented with a series of coloured shapes and have to press the space bar on the keyboard when two shapes match. They are rewarded with a smiley face and a little tune when their responses are correct and a sad face when they are incorrect.

In this activity, the computer is exercising considerable control over the children.

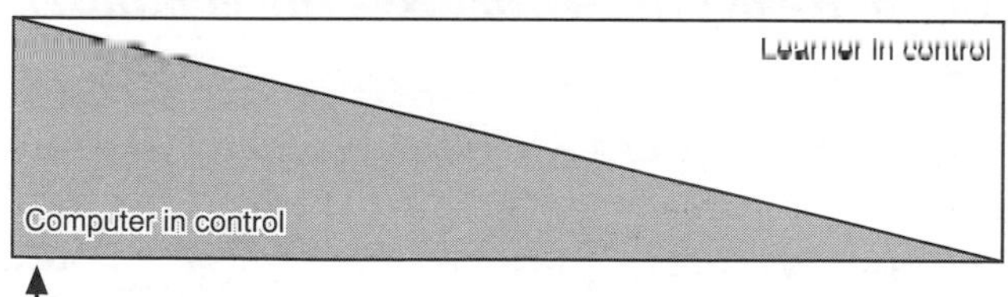

Figure 3.2 Applying the computer-based learning gauge to the colour-matching activity

The computer presents the shapes and colours for the children to match and informs them of their responses. The children are restricted to a key press in response to what the computer decides to show them. The children's thinking and decision-making is at a very low level, as are the IT skills they are required to use. Their control over the computer is minimal.

The picture in Figure 3.3 was created by 4-year-old Kevin using one of the *My World* (SEMERC) files.

Figure 3.3 Kevin's car

My World is a versatile utility program which enables the children to manipulate pictures, text and symbols in a wide range of contexts. Kevin drew his car by moving the mouse pointer over each piece of the car and "dragging" it to the place on the screen where he wanted it to appear. He chose which pieces to use and where they should be placed. When he had finished his picture, one of the 5-year-olds in his class helped him print out his picture on the colour printer.

Where would you place this activity on the computer-based learning gauge? What level of control is being exercised by the child and by the computer? You might like to consider your own response before reading on.

This activity should be placed about midway between the two extremes. The child has some control over the computer but not complete freedom. The "pieces" of the car have been prescribed and the child has no control over their appearance. He does have control over which pieces to use and where they should be positioned. He is having to make decisions which have some degree of open-endedness – the final picture is not predetermined or entirely predictable. The activity also provides him with practice in using the mouse and some, albeit vicarious, experience of using the printer.

Clearly, the pointer on the computer-based learning gauge will be well to the right for this activity (Figure 3.5).

Sadiq exercised almost complete control over the computer. He started with a blank screen, typed in the words he required and placed them where he wanted them to appear using a style he had selected. He worked almost independently of the teacher in an open-ended activity, the outcome being non-prescribed and non-predicted. Sadiq's level of thinking and decision-making was very high. The computer was used by him as a tool to achieve his own objective – producing a piece of writing.

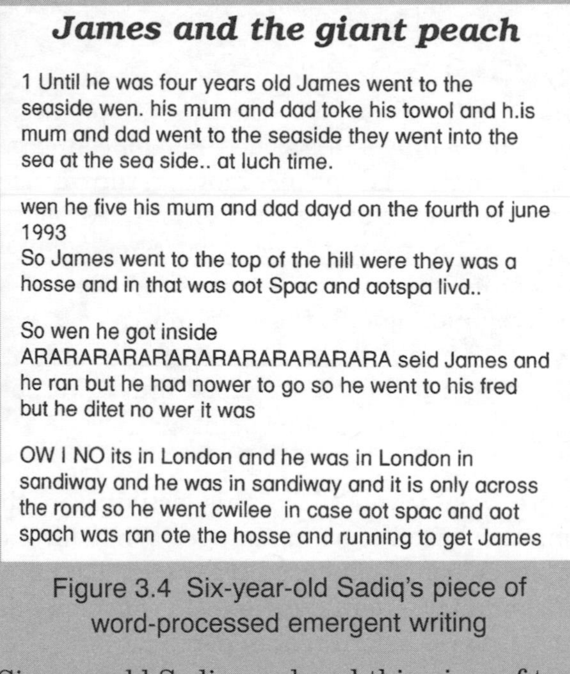

James and the giant peach

1 Until he was four years old James went to the seaside wen. his mum and dad toke his towol and h.is mum and dad went to the seaside they went into the sea at the sea side.. at luch time.

wen he five his mum and dad dayd on the fourth of june 1993
So James went to the top of the hill were they was a hosse and in that was aot Spac and aotspa livd..

So wen he got inside
ARARARARARARARARARARARARA seid James and he ran but he had nower to go so he went to his fred but he ditet no wer it was

OW I NO its in London and he was in London in sandiway and he was in sandiway and it is only across the rond so he went cwilee in case aot spac and aot spach was ran ote the hosse and running to get James

Figure 3.4 Six-year-old Sadiq's piece of word-processed emergent writing

Six-year-old Sadiq produced this piece of text with a word processor. He wrote it straight on to the computer, making use of the computer's editing facilities to insert words and to change the presentation and appearance of the title. *He* thought the title ought to be bigger and bolder than the rest of the writing to make it stand out and be easier to read. When *he* finished his writing, he printed it out and then asked the teacher to help him save his work on his floppy disk, in case he needed to make some changes at a later date.

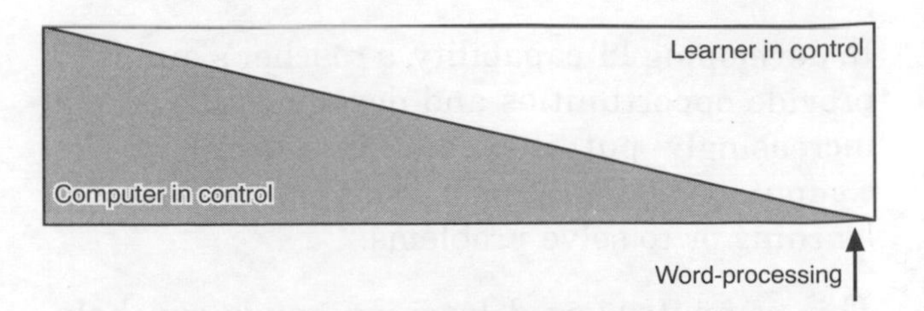

Figure 3.5 Applying the computer-based learning guage to Sadiq's word processing

When the purpose of an activity is to support or enhance work in other areas of the curriculum – to provide experience of colour and shape-matching or to practise spelling, for example – the level of computer control is likely to be very high. Programs which provide this type of low-level reinforcement are usually referred to as "drill and practice" or "content-specific" software. There is a place for this type of computer-based activity provided, of course, this is not the only IT experience the children receive. To develop children's IT capability to the full, they need to be given opportunities to use more intellectually challenging "content-free" software such as word processors, painting and drawing programs or databases where the child's level of control and decision-making potential is quite high. Clearly, this has implications for the teacher in planning work and organising activities which puts control more into the hands of the child.

Content-specific software – the computer as a teacher

There are occasions when the teacher will want the computer to act as an assistant, an additional teacher providing reinforcement, practice or a structured introduction to a new aspect of learning. There is no shortage of software capable of fulfilling this function. Some of it is very well written, based on sound educational principles, and will contribute to children's learning. There is also software which purports to support children's learning which is less than successful – because its entertainment value outweighs its educational worth, because it is dull and uninteresting, or because it has a dubious educational basis.

In selecting software which purports to address specific aspects of children's learning, the following questions might help evaluate its educational potential in the classroom setting:

- What are the children expected to learn by using the program?
- What does the program offer which other approaches do not?
- Is the context motivating for the child?
- To what extent might learning be transferred and applied to other contexts? How could this be assessed?
- Can the teacher (or child) control the content (e.g. can the teacher type in her own word lists, or specify the range of numbers or questions presented)?
- Can the program be tailored to suit the needs of particular children?
- Is there a facility for recording individual children's progress which can be accessed by the teacher?
- What happens if the child makes a mistake? Is he supported or encouraged – does the teacher draw the child's attention to errors and encourage self-correction – does she gloss over some errors and use them to modify the focus and range of questions and problems presented?
- How long are the children required to work at the computer in any one sitting? Can this be adjusted?

Content-free software – the computer as a tool

The most effective way for children to learn about the value of IT is for them to use it purposefully. When Sadiq was making use of the word processor, as a means to an end, the computer was acting as a tool in much the same way as a pen or pencil is used to assist in the writing process.

When using content-free software, such as a word processor, as a tool to assist in children's learning, the following questions might assist in making the most effective use of the software:

- What features and facilities does the software provide which might be used to extend children's learning?
- How easy are these features to use?
- Will the children need to be instructed in their use before or during their use of the software?
- What is the educational purpose underlying the child's use of the software (e.g. To develop IT skills? To learn how to use the software? To use the software as a means to an end? To develop communication skills and knowledge?)?

Developing IT capability – learning about IT

Clearly, one of the main reasons why computers are used in the classroom is for children to learn how to use computers and software. But what exactly should a child be learning? The following pointers provide an overview of the principal IT learning objectives when children are given opportunities to make use of the computer.

Children might be:

- developing skills in the use of IT hardware (keyboard, printers, disk drives, etc.);
- developing skills in the use, and knowledge about the purposes of various types of software;
- learning when and how IT is useful in solving problems or assisting with a task;
- gaining some appreciation of the role of IT in the world.

Opinions vary as to the extent to which children should be expected to become independent in their use of the computer. What is clear, however, is that the more self-reliant children become in making use of the computer, the more likely they are to make use of it – and the more they will develop their skills and confidence in its use.

THE HOBBIT BIY JRR TOLGIN

This is Gandaf theat is a wisud .
and he has a staf .
and he savs the druvs and the
Hobbit . and he leved therem at the
ej ov muk wood .
and they go to beyuns house .
and they go thoow a forist that
had three trols and cachd therem .
and they go thoow sum GOBLIN
tunuls .
and they r go ing to a dragun
cav to get sum TREASURE .
and the dragun ' s name was SMUG .

Figure 3.6 A paragraph about *The Hobbit*, word processed by David and Briony (both aged 6)

Six-year-olds David and Briony worked together on this piece of writing. As part of their normal classroom activities, it was their turn to write a passage about *The Hobbit*, their class story. When they had completed their work, they printed it out themselves, each saved the file on to their own floppy disks and if another pair had not been waiting, they would have closed the computer down and turned it off.

Stage 1	Use of a mouse to position and draw objects on screen
	Use of a concept keyboard to input words, phrases and pictures
Stage 2	Keyboard familiarisation activities
	Activities (e.g. word–processed captions etc.) to apply and extend keyboard knowledge
Stage 3	Activities (e.g. word–processed poems and paragraphs) to increase speed and accuracy in using the keyboard
	How to use the printer
	Loading software
	Starting up and closing down the computer
Stage 4	Saving and loading their own files on to floppy disks
	Replenishing the printer with paper

Table 3.1 Progression in developing IT skills

Progression in the development of IT skills

The basic IT skills which children at Key Stage 1 are capable of developing are outlined in Table 3.1.

Keyboard skills

The keyboard is the most familiar and yet the most difficult of the computer input devices to master. Programs are available which provide practice in locating keys and making use of modifier keys (e.g. shift, caps lock, alt) through animated games (e.g. *Kid Keys* (Ablac)). Spelling practice programs (e.g. *Key Stage 1 Spelling* (Eric)) also provide opportunities for developing skills and speed in locating keys. The most valuable approach to keyboard familiarisation, however, is through making use of the computer for purposeful activities such as word processing a story or desktop publishing a piece of information.

Other input devices

The QWERTY keyboard (named after the arrangement of keys in the top left corner) is only one of the input devices through which information can be communicated directly to a computer. A range of other pieces of equipment, some of which are designed specifically for use by young children or users with physical disabilities, is available for facilitating the inputting process.

Input device	Description	Uses	Comments
Mouse	Hand-held device essential for using the more recent "windows", hard-disk-based computers	Moves a pointer around the screen and selects items from on-screen menus.	Children as young as 2 years can use a mouse (Matthews & Jessel, 1993). Painting programs provide valuable practice in mouse use.
Concept keyboard	A rectangular A3- or A4-sized tablet with 128 pressure-sensitive areas distributed in a grid over its surface	Augments or replaces the conventional keyboard. Overlays of pictures, letters, words or symbols are placed on the tablet which the children then press.	All computers used in schools can use the concept keyboard. Teachers can make their own overlays for use with many educational programs.
Touch screen	A frame placed around a conventional computer monitor which allows children to communicate with the computer by touching parts of the screen	Children can select menu items or draw by touching areas of the screen.	Quite expensive (£250–£300) and there are very few programs which make use of it.
Tracker ball	Similar to an upturned mouse. The user moves the pointer by spinning a ball mounted in a cradle.	Often used by children with manipulative impairment.	Easier to control than a mouse as it stays in one place on the desk. Can replace the mouse on any computer.
Graphics tablet	Similar to the concept keyboard, but far more sensitive. A "stylus" is use to "draw" on or select areas of the computer screen	Used by designers as it is easier to draw accurately than with a mouse.	Relatively expensive and used with specialist (expensive) graphics software.

Table 3.2 Some of the computer input devices suitable for use by children with learning difficulties

There are input devices produced specifically for the needs of disabled children. This aspect will be dealt with later in the chapter under the heading "IT and special educational needs."

Using hardware

As well as developing expertise in the use of the keyboard, children need to develop skills and confidence in the use of the peripheral devices of the computer to help them become independent IT users.

Printers

One of the peripheral first devices children use is the printer. It has been found that children are more likely to identify errors on a printed sheet than on the computer screen. Although work can be printed out at any stage (e.g. after school by the teacher), children who are able to print out their own work, amend it on paper and then return to the machine to edit it are making greater use of the computer as a tool.

Floppy disk drives
Young children should be given the opportunity to access, store and retrieve information which is stored on computer disks. If all the children are provided with their own computer disks and are skilled in saving and loading files, it is possible for them to read, develop and revise written work and drawings produced a year or more later.

Hard disk drives
The more recent generation of computers mostly include hard drives which are built into the computer and hold large amounts of information. Just like a filing cabinet, some sort of system needs to be devised to keep track what is held on the hard drive. It is a wise practice to keep only programs and applications (e.g. the word processor, the database, the graphics package) on the hard drive and save the children's work on to floppy disks. This prevents the hard drive from becoming a depository for large numbers of unknown or unwanted files.

Another option is to open directories or folders for each of the children in the class into which they save their work. Most educational computer companies now market their machines with sets of educational programs and a filing system specifically designed for use by young children (e.g. *Infant Window Box* (RML), *Junior Toolbox* (Xemplar (Acorn and Apple))).

Learning about software and computer applications

For the development of full IT capability children need, not only technical skills in how to use the computer, but knowledge and understanding of when it might be appropriate to use a computer for a task. This is best achieved through purposeful activities in meaningful contexts. In the previous chapter, there was an overview of the types of software and applications which are appropriate for use with Key Stage 1 children. In Chapters 4 and 5, we explore contexts and activities for providing children with relevant experiences related to curriculum areas.

Individual needs and IT

The computer can be used to replace, augment, extend or enhance class teaching. The computer is:

at its best ...

- patient
- non-judgemental
- non-temperamental
- untiring
- consistent in response
- visually stimulating
- uncomplaining
- a valuable assistant

at its worst ...

- impersonal
- unsubtle in its response
- unimaginative in its response
- time consuming
- automatic and unfeeling
- a distraction
- unreliable
- a nuisance

It is incumbent on the teacher to make the most of the computer's virtues and overcome some of its drawbacks. Used appropriately, the computer can become an invaluable asset to the teacher's armoury of strategies for catering for the individual needs of children.

Differentiation for ability

In an ideal world, every child should have an individually devised work programme to cater for his specific needs and learning requirements. The best a hardpressed teacher can do in the mixed-ability classes is to group children according to their needs for some activities. On occasions, she may find time to work with an individual child while the others are engaged in non-teacher-intensive activities. Invariably, she is interrupted.

Differentiation and content-specific software

As this type of software often assumes the role of the teacher, software such as shape-matching or spelling practice programs should be chosen with extreme care and used with careful monitoring. If the teacher can control the level of demand of the software, she can adjust the task to suit the needs of the child.

Differentiation and content-free software

With content-free software where IT is being used as a tool, the teacher and the child have more influence over the way the computer is used. The teacher can differentiate by setting an appropriate task, or by adjusting her level of support. She can, if she wishes, adapt the software to the needs of the child – some word processors and spreadsheets allow the teacher to restrict the range of menu options or incorporate word banks made by the teacher. If the task is not too tightly structured, there is more opportunity for the child to set his own level of demand – leading to differentiation by outcome.

IT and special educational needs

The 1993 Education Act introduced a Code of Practice defining a five-stage model of special educational needs provision. Children identified as having special needs are supposed to have individual educational plans (IEP's) drawn up to address their learning difficulties. The value of computers to support children's learning is well documented (see the Further reading list at the end of this chapter).

Table 3.3 provides some indication of the IT resources which can be used to support children with learning difficulties. The catalogues of specialist suppliers and organisations such as SEMERC and Don Johnston provide information about the software and hardware which is available to support children specific physical, perceptual or cognitive problems.

This table is by no means exhaustive and is intended only to provide an indication of the IT resources which are available. Software packages have been written to help teachers pinpoint the specific learning difficulties which might be affecting a child's performance (e.g. *Cognitive Profiling System* (Chameleon)). SEMERC have produced a file for their *My World* series which helps teachers identify spelling problems in children and assists with the design of a child's IEP (*My World 2: IEP Planner for Spelling*). These should of course never be used as a substitute for professional guidance from specialists. For special educational needs co-ordinators, there is software available to help keep track of pupils with special educational needs and assist with the writing of records and reports (e.g. *SENCo Aid* (SEMERC)).

Groupwork and IT

In the majority of infant schools, children inevitably have to share the computer in order to make maximum use of a scarce and expensive resource. Considerable research has been conducted both in this country and abroad into the effectiveness of group-based collaborative work around the computer yielding some interesting findings:

- Collaborative tasks are more successful for learning than other forms of computer activity (Crook, 1987).
- Pairs of children solve problems more effectively than when they work alone (Kruger, 1993).

Learning difficulty	Comment	IT resources
Reading problems	Reading problems stem from any number of causes: poor vision, visual discrimination problems, lack of maturity, lack of textual experience.	Talking books Visual and auditory discrimination software (e.g. pattern and shape matching) Structured language programs
Writing problems	Problems with writing can occur through difficulties with co-ordination or from cognitive difficulties in relating symbols to sounds or words. It can also stem from lack of experience with reading.	Handwriting practice programs Talking word processors Rebus symbol-writing software (e.g. *Writing with Symbols* (Widgit)) Spelling checkers (pocket or word-processor based) Predictive word processors (e.g. *Co:writer* (Don Johnston))
Problems with mathematics	Problems with mathematics are often related to poor understanding of mathematical concepts stemming from insufficient first-hand experience. Perceptual difficulties or problems with memory can be contributory factors.	Number familiarisation software LOGO Maths practice software (with caution) (See Chapter 5)
Dyslexia	Dyslexia relates to otherwise able children who have difficulty with reading, writing and some aspects of mathematics. Much of their difficulty is related to problems with short-term memory and the storage, organisation and retrieval of information.	Talking books Talking word processors Visual and auditory discrimination software Spelling programs NB Spelling checkers are not of great use dyslexics
Visual impairment		Word processors with large text displays Talking books and encyclopaedias Talking word processors Braille readers
Hearing impairment	Hearing loss can be temporary or specific to certain frequencies as opposed to a general overall reduction in hearing	Practically any software which makes use of the screen to communicate information
Physical impairment	Ranging from minor co-ordination problems through to paraplegia	Predictive word processor (cuts down the number of key presses required) Input devices (e.g. switched inputs operated by restricted movements of the hand, head or eyes)

Table 3.3 Some of the IT resources which are available for use with children with learning difficulties

- Pairs of children work more consistently and accurately than individuals on computer tasks such as word processing (Paoletti, 1995).
- Collaborative learning works most effectively when the task requires joint decision-making, rather than when an activity requires children to independently take turns at using the keyboard (Blaye & Light, 1995).
- Younger children work better in pairs, whereas older children work better in threes (Blease & Cohen, 1990).

Despite having to exercise healthy scepticism when interpreting research findings in the classroom, there does appear to be a convincing body of evidence to suggest that, when activities are organised to encourage children to collaborate on an activity, the resultant learning is deeper. A great deal depends of course on the nature of the tasks and the quality of the relationships between the children concerned. The public display of the work on a computer screen, and in some ways the laborious process of typing, seems to encourage children to be more conciliatory and collaborative when writing at the computer. This provides unrivalled opportunities for children to develop their communication and social skills of speaking and listening.

Talk and the computer

Infant teachers are very aware of the importance to children of the provision of good speaking and listening activities. If the computer is used carefully, it can provide situations which encourage talk, collaborative decision-making and the consideration of others' viewpoints. Research into the value of the computer for generating talk suggests:

- Mixed-ability groups produce more discussion than same-ability groups (Hill & Brown, 1988).
- The teacher should structure the task to ensure all children are able to participate by changing their roles during an activity (e.g. taking turns at the keyboard) (Sheingold *et al.*, 1984).
- Teacher intervention is critical to the encouragement of more complex levels of discussion at the computer (Hill & Brown, 1988).
- A great deal of computer software is not designed to encourage purposeful discussion (Jackson *et al.*, 1986).

Hill and Brown's (1988) study with 6- and 7-year-olds working together on the *Granny's Garden* (4mation) adventure program highlights the importance of providing software which stimulates purposeful discussion. It also focuses attention on the value of careful teacher intervention to encourage more complex levels of talking and, by implication, thinking.

Gender, equal opportunities and IT

In the field of IT evidence indicates that:

- girls learn more in co-operative learning situations than with competitive activities (Johnson *et al.* 1985);
- the gender mix of groups of younger children is less important to learning than it is with older children (Haywood & Wray, 1988);
- when putting a more experienced child with one who is less experienced, the less experienced child learns more if the more experienced 'mentor' has a clear idea of his role and the teacher interacts occasionally to reinforce this role (Underwood *et al.*, 1990).

Although experience and research suggest that gender mix is less important with younger children, attention needs to be paid to the stereotyping of attitudes with young children. Anita Straker (1989) found that when 5-year-olds were asked who they expected to be good at using the computer, both girls and boys responded that they expected boys to be better than girls. Research indicates that as activities become increasingly more competitive, girls are likely to participate less and less. Research findings also indicate that, whereas girls tend to be more successful in language-related activities (e.g. word processing), boys tend to do better at tasks related to spatial awareness (e.g. LOGO). Pairing boys with girls can have benefits, though research suggests that boys are less inclined to benefit when working with girls on language activities, whereas girls benefit when working with boys on spatial tasks (i.e. boys don't listen, whereas girls do! Hughes & Greenough, 1989).

In some classrooms, the computer is made available only to children who have finished all their other work. As a consequence, more able children tend to receive more contact with the computer than those who are less academic. IT is particularly suited to addressing the needs of children with learning difficulties, particularly when work or software is targeted to address specific learning problems. When planning and organising activities, teachers need to be aware of the entitlement of all children in all areas of the curriculum to make use of IT.

Finally, the attitudes and actions of teachers must be considered. Children are highly susceptible to the influence of gender role models. Perhaps, the next time the computer fails to function properly, Mrs Smith ought to be sent for, rather than Mr Jones.

Summary

In this chapter we have seen how important it is to monitor the levels of control present in computer-based learning situations. The greater the level of control the child has over the computer, the more opportunity he has to develop his IT capability.

We have also examined how children learn with IT, through IT and what children need to learn about IT. Although the computer can support the learning of children with special educational needs, it is important that the teacher selects appropriate software and ensures the tasks and her or the computer's support and responses are matched to the needs of the child.

In organising groupwork, the computer can encourage real collaborative learning and stimulate valuable discussion. The constitution of these groups and their management is critical to the success of this type of activity.

Far from computers seeking to replace the teacher, the teacher's role is central to the effective use of IT in the classroom.

References

Blaye, A. & Light, P. (1995) Collaborative Problem Solving with Hypercard: The Influence of Peer Interaction on Planning and Information Handling Strategies; in O'Malley, C. (ed.) *Computer Supported Collaborative Learning*; Springer Verlag/NATO

Blease, D. & Cohen, L. (1990) *Coping with Computers*; Paul Chapman

Crook, C. (1987) Computers in the Classroom; in Rutkowska, J. C. & Crook, C. (eds) *Computers, Cognition and Development*; John Wiley & Sons.

Haywood, S. & Wray, D. (1988) Using Tray, a text Reconstruction Program with Top Infants; *Educational Review*, vol. 40, pp. 29–39

Hill, A. & Brown, A. (1988) Talk and the Microcomputer: An Investigation in the Infant Classroom; *Reading*, vol. 22 (1), pp. 61–9

Hughes, M. & Greenough, P. (1989) Gender and Social Interaction in Early LOGO Use; in Collins, J. H., Estes, N., Gattis, W. D. & Walker, D. (eds) *Proceedings of the Sixth International Conference on Technology and Education*, Vol. 1; CEP

Jackson, A., Fletcher, B. & Messer, D. J. (1986) A Survey of Microcomputer Use and Provision in Primary Schools; *Journal of Computer Assisted Learning*, vol. 2, pp. 45–55

Johnson, R. T., Johnson, D. W. & Stanne, M. B. (1985) Effects of Co-operative, Competitive and Individualistic Goal Structures on Computer-assisted Instruction; *Journal of Educational Psychology*, vol. 77, pp. 668–77

Kruger, A. C. (1993) Peer Collaboration: Conflict, Co-operation or Both? *Social Development*, vol. 2, pp. 165–82

Matthews, J. & Jessel J. (1993) Very Young Children and Electronic Paint: The Beginning of Drawing with Traditional Media and Computer Paintbox; *Early Years*, vol. 13(2), pp. 15–22

Paoletti, G. (1995) Peer Interaction and Writing: The Process of Revision; in O'Malley, C. (ed.) *Computer Supported Collaborative Learning*; Springer Verlag/ NATO

Sheingold, K., Hawkins, J. & Char, C. (1984) I'm the Thinkist, You're the Typist: The Interaction of Technology and the Social Life of Classrooms; *Journal of Social Issues*, vol. 40 (3), pp. 49–61

Straker, A. (1989) *Children Using Computers*; Nash Pollock Publishing

Underwood, G., McCaffrey, M. & Underwood, J. (1990) Gender Differences in Co-operative Computer-based Language Tasks; *Educational Research*, vol. 32, pp. 44–9

Further reading on special educational needs and IT

Hawkridge, D. & Vincent, T. (1992) *Learning Difficulties and Computers*; Jessica Kingsley Publications

McKeown, S. (ed.) (1992) *IT Support and Specific Learning Difficulties*; NCET

McKeown, S. (ed.) (1993) *Dyslexia and Mathematics*; NCET

Singleton, C. (ed.) (1994) *Computers and Dyslexia*; Dyslexia Resource Centre

4 IT activities and curriculum: the core subjects

What this chapter is about

This chapter deals with the three core subjects of the UK curriculum in turn and indicates:

- ways in which existing subject-based activities can be supported or enhanced through the use of IT;
- suggestions for extending classroom activities in the core subjects with IT;
- how children's IT capability can be developed through the core subjects.

IT strands which are covered in this chapter include:

- word processing and desktop publishing,
- databases and data handling,
- monitoring through data logging.

Finding out about software

Although software titles are mentioned in this chapter, they by no means constitute a definitive list. It is the way software is used by teachers and children which dictates its educational value. Teachers often ask how they can find out about software. As with most ideas in teaching, information reaches the classroom through many diverse routes:

- personal recommendation – teachers sharing ideas at meetings or socially;
- visiting other schools – and "borrowing" good ideas;
- software catalogues – mailed regularly to school and sometimes filed away for safe keeping;
- getting catalogues or directories from generalist software dealers – these list a wide range of software with brief descriptions under headings (see Appendix III for names and addresses);
- contacting the major educational computer manufacturers for their approved software lists;
- dropping into the local IT education centre, where these still exist;
- going on INSET courses – to pick up what's new, or to find new ways of using existing software;
- attending conferences – e.g. the BETT Conference held in London every January is the Mecca for all educational software producers.

Some software companies (e.g. Sherston) will send copies of their programs on approval so you can "try before you buy".

English and IT

As would be expected, most IT activities which are associated with English contribute to the development of IT capabilities in *communicating information*. As will be shown, with careful planning activities can be organised which simultaneously develop children's skills and knowledge in English and in IT.

Speaking and listening

Supporting and enhancing speaking and listening activities with IT

Early years teachers appreciate the educational value of reading aloud to children. They realise it not only introduces children to the idea of how books work and the pleasure that can be gained from listening to stories, but also the benefit for children in hearing formal sentence structure and imaginative vocabulary. One problem associated with reading aloud to a group is that the children do not always see the pages which are being read to them.

Audio tapes and listening units

Many teachers employ IT through the use of audio story tapes and listening units. Groups of children wearing headphones listen to a story, sometimes following the words in a book. Children who are less proficient with reading often have difficulty keeping pace with the reader or may ignore the text entirely.

Talking books

"Talking books" are computerised versions of picture books which make use of the computer's ability to interact with the user. Most talking books highlight each word on the screen as it is being read. Children can move a pointer to individual words to hear these being enunciated in a natural voice or can hear the text read as many times as they wish. The relationship between text and sound is thereby reinforced visually and aurally. Most talking books (though not all) are provided in CD ROM, owing to the enormous amounts of computer memory which digitised speech requires. When selecting software with a speech option, the following questions might prove useful.

- Are the talking books compatible with the school's existing reading scheme or approach?
- What opportunities are provided for children to interact with the text – e.g. will the computer "sound" individual words indicated by the children?
- Do the illustrations and animated scenes contribute to the enjoyment of the book, or do they distract attention from the story or the reading of the text?

Extending opportunities for Speaking and listening through IT

Collaborative discussion

As has been mentioned in the previous chapter, computer-based activities, if carefully structured, can create opportunities for children to engage in genuine collaborative tasks. This can be at any level of complexity or linguistic demand, such as:

- simple shared tasks – for example, two children writing a poem together, each contributing alternate lines;
- a group of three children having to decide on the content of their contribution to the class story;
- a group of children making decisions about the next course of action in an adventure program;
- a group of children deciding the most appropriate way to gather information to answer an enquiry which they have devised – e.g. "People jump further if they are taller";
- the whole class planning the content and structure for the class newsletter to parents, and various editorial teams then working together on different aspects and contributions.

The following factors are critical to the success of organising collaborative work around the computer to encourage talk.

- The focus of the task. Do the children really know what is expected of them and that they must take account of everyone's views before a decision is taken?
- The extent to which designated roles are changed during the activity. It often arises that the child who is in control of the keyboard is the one who dominates. Making sure all the children have a turn at the keyboard can help reduce this potential problem.

Digitising children's speech

There are some story writing packages (e.g. *Storybook Theatre* (TAG)) which allow the user to incorporate their own speech with the words and pictures on screen. The children can, if they wish, create their own talking books or add their voices to parts of stories. This clearly opens up all sorts of opportunities for the development of children's speaking and listening skills. There is, however, a catch.

Computerised sound uses large amounts of memory. A floppy disk would be unlikely to hold more than 2 minutes' worth of speech, together with the text for the story to which it relates. As a consequence, this type of software usually requires a computer with a hard disk drive. A far more cost-effective solution is to use a tape recorder and provide opportunities for children to record their own taped stories for each other.

Reading

In the previous section, we have already seen how talking books provide opportunities for children to hear and see a book being read to them. Some reading scheme publishers now provide software or CD ROM packages to support children's learning.

Supporting and enhancing reading with IT

Unlike a book, a computer can be made to emphasise, to animate, to respond, to speak and, in some cases, to listen. Computer-based reading activities include the following.

- Pre-reading activities, such as sequencing, and shape- and colour-matching. The *My World 2* early learning package (SEMERC), for example, includes a set of activities in which children match objects, find the odd one out and practise letter recognition.
- Letter recognition and alphabetical ordering. *Alphadog* (AVP) is an example of a piece of software in which the children have to direct a dog to find letters in the correct order within a pre-set time limit.
- Phonic reinforcement activities. A wide range of software is available to support children's learning of phonics. Some rely on children identifying the initial, middle and final letter sounds of words and images (e.g. *Letters and Pictures* (Chalksoft)) while others include digitised speech to reinforce the sound-letter relationship (e.g. *Kid Phonics* (Ablac)).
- Word building. *Read Right Away 1 2 3 4* (HS Software) provides a series of activities in computer arcade game format to practise word building with consonant blends and vowel digraphs.
- Word recognition and sight vocabulary exercises. *Play and Read* (Prisma) provides a set of four activities, one of which helps children build their sight vocabulary.
- Sequencing words or phrases into sentences. With *Panache* (SEMERC), the children move "cards" containing words or phrases around the screen to construct meaningful sentences.
- Word games and word familiarisation activities. *Let's Play with Words* (Torcoed) provides a set of six activities in which the children have to identify words and non-words, fill spaces in sentences, match similar sounding words, correctly sequence a nursery rhyme, and make words.

As with most resources, the effectiveness of any piece of software is dependent upon the way it is used and the extent to which it is integrated into a systematic programme of language development. Opinions vary over the educational value and effectiveness of some of the above drill-and-practice exercises with the computer. It must be borne in mind that although such activities can provide low-level reinforcement of basic skills, they rarely provide opportunities for children to use higher order thinking skills or acquire knowledge needed for developing IT capability (see Chapter 3).

Extending reading activities through IT

The following resources are examples of the way that computers can be used to develop reading skills.

- Computer-based language activities. For example, *Podd* (ESM) is a program with a long history. The children have to discover which actions Podd can perform by typing in verbs to complete the sentence *Podd can* … . This program has sparked off many imaginative activities in infant classrooms. A set of ideas cards has been produced to accompany the program.
- Adventure programs, in which the children have to read the text to solve riddles and problems, and make decisions to determine the way the story progresses (e.g. *Granny's Garden* (4mation), *Elf Tales* (Sherston)).
- Software packages which make use of speech, visual images and text. *Multimedia Flashcards* (TAG) presents words and pictures on the screen. The children can listen to the words being read aloud and can record their own voices, provided sufficient memory is available (see above).

- Talking books, animated story books which allow the reader some control over the way the text is presented and read and which have animated pictures (e.g. *Living Books* (Broderbund), *Oxford Reading Tree Talking Books* (Sherston)). Medwell (1995) has shown that children, particularly boys, who use talking books were more accurate with their reading than children who rely on teacher instruction alone.

In addition to software written specifically to support reading, practically any program which encourages children to purposefully engage with text could be used to enhance the children's reading skills, including word processors and software aimed at supporting writing skills.

Writing

A computer can be used both directly and indirectly to support children's development of writing skills. An indirect application of software, for example, is when children have been involved in working through an adventure program and then produce a piece of writing about their imaginary experiences. Other indirect uses of the computer to develop writing include:

- using computer-based information sources, such as databases or encyclopaedias, to provoke, support or inform factual writing;
- condensing information for inclusion in a database;
- following up work on computer simulations (e.g. *Zoo Keeper* (TAG));
- producing written work inspired by "reading" talking books.

Supporting and enhancing children's writing with IT

As with reading, most aspects of children's writing development can be supported or enhanced through the use of a computer. Examples include:

- Assisting with children's learning of correct letter formation and handwriting. *Write-It* (AVP), for example, draws lower and upper case letters slowly on the screen for children to copy.
- *My First Words* (CSH) is an example of a computerised word bank, similar to the Breakthrough to Literacy folders which were once used extensively by infant schools.
- Packages which combine text and symbols for supporting emergent writing. *Writing with Pictures* (Widget) is one example which enables children to write using a combination of words and Rebus symbols (picture symbols representing words). A speech option allows the pieces of "writing" to be read back.
- Spelling practice and vocabulary extension programs such as *An Eye for Spelling* (ESM) provide systematic spelling practice.

The type of software which a school uses to support children's writing and the way it is used in the classroom is largely dependent upon the school's policy towards writing. A school which places greater emphasis on children's emergent writing is likely to value different software tools to one which prefers a highly structured key-words approach.

> The Year 2 class of one urban infant school uses a BBC B computer to continuously run a spelling program (*Starspell Plus* (Fisher-Marriott)). The children work systematically through a series of spelling lists to build their spelling vocabulary through the Look–Cover–Write–Check approach. The teacher adds her own word lists to those included in the computer when she recognises particular problems arising. The children use the program on a rolling rota basis so that each child practises her spelling at least once a fortnight. The classroom also has an Acorn Archimedes computer which is used for more creative IT work.

Extending the range of writing activities through IT

Some of the ways in which the computer can be used to extend children's writing include:

- Helping children to write text through pointing at pictures or symbols with a concept keyboard, touch screen or mouse pointer. Most educational word processors include options for receiving input from a concept keyboard. Teachers can create their own overlays to enable children to enter text by pressing pictures, symbols, phrases, words or letters on the keyboard.
- Inserting whole words and phrases into children's word processing from word banks which have be created by the teacher (e.g. *Full Phase* (SEMERC))
- Making use of talking word processors which read back what the children have written or sound out each word as it is typed in (e.g. *Talking Textease* (Softease)). The Somerset Talking Computer Project (see Miles, 1994) has found there are particular advantages for children with learning difficulties in having a device which will help them associate text with spoken words in this way.
- Having a word processor which predicts and inserts the most likely word after only one or two key presses (e.g. *PAL* (Lander)). The use of this type of program cuts down the number of key presses by up to 50% – a boon for children with restricted movement or poor co-ordination.
- Writing illustrated story books or newspaper reports using text template packages which provide a ready-made framework. *EasyBook* (TAG) and *BookMaker 2* (Resource) present children with a book format into which they can type their own stories and select suitable pictures. The books can then be read on screen or printed out and made into high-quality conventional books.
- Producing interactive presentations using multimedia packages for text, sound and graphics (e.g. *Ultima* (SEMERC), *Hyperstudio* (TAG).

Figure 4.1 A page from class 1's Hyperstudio story

Class 1 (a mixed Reception/Year 1 class) had never used a multimedia package before. The 5-year-olds decided to write a story for the Reception children. To save time and to ensure some sort of consistency, the teacher set up a series of pages with pictures. A different pair of children was responsible for the text on each of the pages. The level of detail on each of the pages reflects the children's abilities with language, though the teacher assisted with editing after the children had typed in their work to help both the writers and the readers with their language skills.

Educational word processors

There is a confusingly large number of word-processing packages marketed for school use. Some educational word processors are fairly restricted and do not offer the full range of features which children might need to use to gain the most from their word processing. A word processor must not only meet the needs of the children at the time, but have the potential to challenge and extend the children's IT capabilities. The responses to the following questions provide an indication of the accessibility and potential of a word processing package for young children.

- How simple and reliable is the menu and mouse selection system?

- Can the menus and other features be tailored by the teacher to suit the needs of the children?
- Can the text size be adjusted on screen to ease reading and writing?
- Are sans serif fonts displayed on screen for younger users?
- Does it include full editing facilities (cutting, pasting, moving and block delete)?
- Can pictures be pasted into the text?
- Can the package be used with a concept keyboard or other input devices?
- Does it offer speech to read back children's work? Can it read each word as it is typed, or does it only read completed texts?
- How easy is the procedure for loading and saving text files?
- Is there a word bank or spell checking facility? How easy is it to use?
- To what extent has the word-processing package been trialed with young children and their teachers?

Some professional word-processing packages (e.g. *Claris Works*) provide extra utilities (e.g. *Easyworks*) to help younger children or those with learning, sensory or perceptual difficulties. Such aids provide simplified menu systems which enable even the youngest children to make use of the more powerful features of such word-processing packages. These include spell checking, full editing and formating features (page numbering, headers and footers, graphics importing). A major advantage of using a tailored version of a more powerful package is that children can gradually be introduced to its more complex features as they progress though school. It will also mean that the children's work can be loaded into other text-processing packages (sometimes on different types of computers) at any later stage.

Learning about IT through English activities

Clearly, the major contribution which English activities can offer the development of children's IT capability is in the enhancement of keyboard skills and increased knowledge of the ways in which computers can handle text. Children will realise that once some text has been written, it becomes the start of the editing and redrafting process rather than an end-point. More significantly, they will come to appreciate that through editing text, the ideas which it represents can be reworked also.

Children will inevitably want to print out their own work. Having a pristine piece of writing which is free from smudges and crabbed handwriting is often a reward in itself. Training the children in the use of the printer and the saving and loading of their own work not only develops the children's IT capability but releases the teacher for more important work.

Mathematics and IT

If we assume that mathematics is a tool which helps us view the world in a more precise manner and provides us with "a means of communication which is powerful, concise and unambiguous" (Cockcroft, 1982, p. 1), then our teaching of mathematics to young children ought to reflect this.

Developing mathematical thinking with IT

With all stages of mathematical learning (including postgraduate level!), the use of practical equipment to help develop mental models and to build understanding is essential. The translation of concrete experiences into personalised internal models which can be then used to manipulate ideas without the need for physical equipment is called the abstraction process. This process should never be hurried. All learners need time and a range of experiences to help develop their mathematical understanding. The greater the variety of contexts in which a learner experiences a new idea, the more enduring and robust will be her understanding. Used carefully, a computer can assist in the learning process by helping children to translate physical experiences into internalised mental structures.

Pamela Liebeck proposes a four-stage process towards abstraction based on Bruner's modes of thought representation:

E – *experience* with physical objects

L – spoken *language* that describes that experience

P – *pictures* that represent the experience

S – written *symbols* that generalise the experience

(Liebeck, 1984, p. 16)

The computer should never replace children's direct experience with physical objects. It can assist with the development of language, provided activities are structured appropriately. But the most useful role for the computer in the abstraction process comes in its ability to present pictures and symbols. For young children, visual imagery is a powerful medium for thinking. Children are better able to represent and manipulate ideas in picture form than in symbolic abstract form. Used with care, the computer can assist with the most difficult stage in the development of mathematical understanding – helping children to associate their visually represented ideas with abstract symbols.

Supporting and enhancing the teaching of mathematics with IT

As with language development, the extent to which IT contributes to the mathematics curriculum is largely dependent upon which aspects of the mathematics curriculum a school values. Most areas of the mathematics curriculum are supported in some way by computer software. So, how should a teacher go about choosing software to support, enhance or extend her teaching of mathematics?

Pre-number activities

Pre-number activities, such as sorting, classifying, labelling, comparing and ordering, provide children with the all-important foundation concepts on which they build their understanding of mathematical ideas. Children need to work with physical objects to help establish and build their understanding of the relationships between objects. Carefully structured activities which systematically impose more order to children's initial random activities help lay the foundations for a mathematical approach to organising, quantifying and representing physical experience.

Whilst the computer cannot replace physical experience, it can assist in the process of developing strategies for organising, quantifying and representing similar experiences in picture form.

Figure 4.2 *Freddy Teddy* is an appealing elementary maths practice program

Freddy Teddy (Topologika) is one example of the many programs which present situations on the screen for children to practise their sorting, classifying and ordering skills. In this case, the children have to help Freddy match objects by colour and size.

Number work (including algebra)

Numeration, whereby quantities or sets of objects are represented by an arbitrary abstract symbol, is fundamental to all mathematics. Carefully chosen software can assist in this process once children have reached the language/picture/symbol stage. Talking software can reinforce the link between number name, number of items and numeral. On the computer screen, randomly organised objects will animate themselves into orderly sets or groups and be counted. A set of objects can literally be replaced by a numeral, and vice versa.

Janet teaches a Reception class in a suburban infant school. The class shares a BBC B computer and an Archimedes A 3020 with the other Reception class. When it is her turn to have the BBC B, Janet uses some early maths practice software to help reinforce the children's understanding of basic number concepts. One of the children's favourite pieces of software, *Number Snap* (MEP Infant Maths), helps children match sets of objects to large numerals presented on the screen. Janet integrates this activity with a range of practical activities in which the children sort, classify and order sets of objects and assign numerals to sets.

Place value

Interestingly, there are very few programs which support the teaching of the concept of place value. Those which do exist seem to be reworking of BBC B software which has been available for some time. Some of the original MEP programs (e.g. *Number in the National Curriculum* (ESM)) which were issued in the early 1980s still provide some interesting, if a little dated, activities.

Number operations

Practice and reinforcement for the number operations (addition, subtraction, multiplication and division) are well supported with software. It ranges from drill-and-practice "sums" tests to more imaginative software that helps to reinforce children's understanding of the concepts underlying the operations. An example that fits into the latter category is *Connections* (Sherston). The children are required to model equations (sums) in a number of different ways – using pictures, sets, scales, tallies and so on. The program can also be used to provide practice with money and fractions.

Simulations and role play

Simulations allow the children to participate in role-playing activities under the direction of the computer. *Supermarket* (Resource) uses the context of supermarket shopping to reinforce understanding of money transactions. For older children, *Funfair* (Northern Micromedia) uses the fairground as the situation for practising number and money skills.

Data handling

Data handling is an area of mathematical activity which is most closely associated with IT and is specifically mentioned in the National Curriculum Orders for mathematics. As has been mentioned (see Chapter 2), the advantage in having the computer drawing the graphs is that by taking the chore out of drawing and colouring the charts, the children's attention can be directed more towards data gathering and interpretation.

There are several graph-drawing programs available for most types of computer. *Pictogram* (Kudlian) helps children appreciate the relationship between the solid bars on a bar chart and the numbers they represent by allowing a teacher or child to switch the chart display from picture-blocks to coloured blocks or solid bars.

When the mixed Reception and Year 1 class was studying animals, they decided to find out how many different pets there would be if every child brought theirs to school. Finding it difficult to remember who had put up their hand for each animal mentioned, the teacher suggested they use the computer to help them. Using *Picturepoint* (Longman Logotron), the computer displayed boxes showing each of their pets (apart from Lucy's guinea pigs). Each child in turn came to the computer and clicked the mouse pointer over the picture(s) of their pet(s). The computer responded by making the noise of the pet and adding another block to the top of a graph. After all the children had entered their information, they could see immediately which was the most popular pet and, by clicking the mouse pointer over the appropriate column, the computer spoke the number it represented.

Before deciding to make use of more sophisticated IT data-handling software, the teacher must decide what educational objectives she has for using the computer. If the sole purpose is for children to draw, analyse and interpret graphs, then a graph-drawing package such as those described above would be sufficient. If, on the other hand, the objectives are for children to manipulate the data –to sort, classify and select categories and to look for patterns and trends in the data – then it might be worthwhile for the children to use a database or spreadsheet package.

Just before Sports Day, the 32 children in Year 2 of a primary school were interested in finding out about their sporting accomplishments. Various hypotheses were floated, including "Children with long legs are better jumpers". One group devised a test to evaluate this theory and then entered the information into a computer database (*Junior Pinpoint* (Longman Logotron)) with the help of a parent to check for errors.

Being able to sort, select and graph sets of children who have long legs and children who can jump the greatest distance enabled them to search for patterns in their data.

The teacher helped put the children's names in order of the length of their legs and then they printed out the graph to see whether children with the shortest legs jumped less far than those with longer legs. Jack (Jk) is the best jumper, but his legs are middle-sized. Polly (Py) has the shortest legs, but her jump is almost as far as that of Jon's (Jn), who has the longest legs. The children decided the length of their legs had no effect on the distance they could jump. They then went on to test other hypotheses.

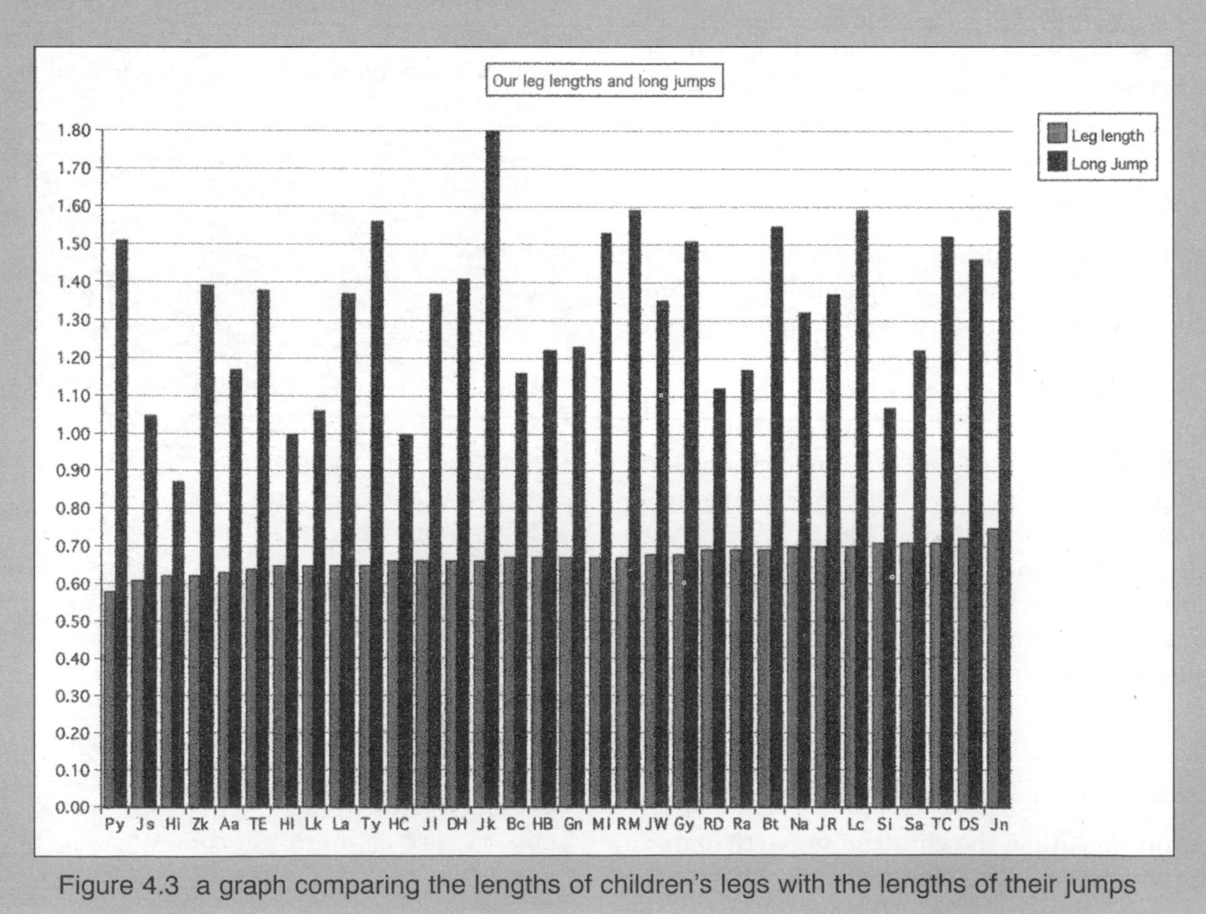

Figure 4.3 a graph comparing the lengths of children's legs with the lengths of their jumps

Shape, space and measures

Infant teachers appreciate the importance of raising children's awareness of shape and space in helping children to learn about their immediate environment. A systematic study of shape and space is as important to an appreciation of mathematics as is the study of number, as the Ancient Greeks demonstrated. Measuring creates one of the links between shape and number and can provide children with a useful modelling tool for the representation of number relationships. The number-line is one example of this.

When it comes to computer support for shape and space activities, there is a mixed bag of software available. This ranges from undemanding shape-naming programs to more creative software that allows children to investigate spatial relationships. *Albert's House* (Resource), for example, encourages the children to explore a house, finding the position of items in relation to other objects, thereby giving practice in the use of positional language (under, beside, on top, etc.). Several of the *My World* files (SEMERC) provide experience with shape positioning, logic and translation (e.g. *Rotate, Read and Do, Shape Pictures, Tessellation*).

But is probably through LOGO turtle graphics that the greatest appreciation of shape, space and measurement can be gained through the use of IT.

Extending the range of mathematical activities through IT – LOGO

With LOGO turtle graphics, the children control a turtle's movements about the screen by giving it a series of commands, such as FORWARD 20 or LEFT 30. As the turtle moves, it leaves a trail. In this way the children can instruct the turtle to draw on screen.

The power of LOGO lies in its programming potential. Children are able to teach the turtle new commands by putting together a series of instructions in a procedure which the turtle will follow. By combining a series of procedures, the turtle can be made to draw a quite complex scene. The children, in this way, become computer programmers and problem solvers while using the turtle to explore the space represented by the computer screen.

LOGO enables children to investigate space mathematically. Through simple challenges, either set by the teacher or generated by the children themselves, they set out to solve problems through trial and improvement. Seymour Papert, the instigator of LOGO, suggests the turtle provides children with "an object to think with" (Papert, 1980) – a link between the experiential, pictorial and symbolic representation (see above). Teachers who have used LOGO with young children have been surprised by the ease and rapidity with which children are able to use quite large numbers in their investigations (see Straker, 1989, p. 91 and Blythe, 1990).

Two 6-year-olds, Ben and Nathan, were using LOGO to draw a tree to go with their picture of a house. They were experiencing difficulty getting the size right.

Ben: Try 100.
Nathan: That's no good. It's bigger.
Ben: What was it … how big?
Nathan: Err … 70, I think.
Ben: Shall we try 70 again?
Nathan: Yeh, all right. [*Types in.*]
Ben: Yeh. It *is* too big.
Nathan: We could try 50, that's smaller.
Ben: Yeh or 47, that's smaller
Nathan: Or 40 anything.
Ben: Do 47. [*Nathan types in 47.*] Yeh, that's better.

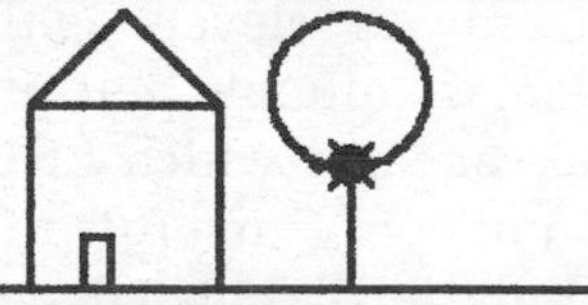

Figure 4.4 Ben and Nathan's LOGO picture

Nathan is considered to be of average ability and Ben receives additional help with reading and number work.

For Ben and Nathan, numbers have a special significance. They can relate them to their mental images of the turtle moving and turning. They enjoy LOGO and spend a large amount of their free time using the computer.

Not every child finds LOGO turtle graphics interesting. Another way to stimulate interest in mathematics is through the use of adventure programs which have a mathematical content (e.g. *Red Riding Hood* (Selective), Puff (ESM), *Maths Dragons* (Coombe Valley), *Maths Adventure* (Cosmos)). The problems that are presented can either be solved through discussion at the computer, can become the focus of a class-based activity or can spark off a whole series of mathematical activities away from the computer.

Mathematical activities and the development of IT capability – learning about IT with mathematics

The most significant contribution mathematics can make to the development of children's IT skills and knowledge is in data handling. Provided the task for which the database is used is appropriate, children will gain valuable experience in understanding how IT can make data handling easier. If the task becomes more convoluted or arduous with IT than it would have been without it, the question must be asked – why use a database?

LOGO programming provides a unique opportunity for young children to discover how computers operate. Although few will go on to become computer programmers, having some insight into the way a computer carries out a sequence of instructions, and that computers are only as "clever" as the people who program them, is valuable in itself. The foundation skills and concepts which LOGO programming gives is not only useful in itself, but provides foundation knowledge for a wide range of related LOGO-based activities with music, animation, multimedia, computer modelling or control. This helps develop children's IT capability by putting the control of the computer and its application into their hands.

Science and IT

As with mathematics, National Curriculum documentation for science specifically mentions the use of IT for sorting, handling and manipulating data. The goal of science education is to help the children develop the skills, knowledge and understanding to view the world scientifically.

> Science for primary children is ... an activity which provides opportunity for children:
>
> - to explore the natural and man made world around them
> - to test out the ideas they have and develop them so that they become more useful in explaining what they find in their exploration
> - to develop skills and attitudes required to gather and use evidence in forming and testing ideas
>
> (Harlen, 1985, p. 12)

With younger children, the starting point for scientific activity has to be the world around them. Their science work should develop their knowledge and understanding to make scientific sense of their immediate environment and to acquire the skills to test their ideas and predictions.

Whilst computer software, particularly that found on CD ROM, is capable of taking aspects of familiar and unfamiliar experience and presenting them in highly attractive and stimulating ways, teachers of Key Stage 1 children should guard against the temptation to replace direct experience with computerised versions of reality. Children develop their scientific skills of enquiry through direct first-hand experience. There are some situations, however, where the computer can contribute to or extend the opportunities which the teacher can provide.

Supporting and enhancing the teaching and learning of science with IT

IT support for the learning of knowledge in science comes principally in two forms – the presentation of information which the children have gathered for themselves and the use of ready-made information sources such as databases or simulations.

Data handling and scientific enquiry

All work in science ought to be aimed at developing the children's skills of scientific investigation and enquiry. The constructivist principle which underlies the Science National Curriculum is that children build their understanding of the world from their experiences. Rather than imposing an accepted "scientific" explanation, the teacher should strive to present situations which provide opportunities for children to compare their understanding and explanations with reality. At times, their explanations and understanding will need to be challenged; at other times, their awareness will need to be extended or broadened. To assist in the development of soundly based conceptions, children should learn the skills of systematic, interpretative enquiry, to ensure that their observations are accurate and consistent.

IT can assist in this process by providing tools to help record, systematise and analyse children's findings.

Such activities help children appreciate the ways botanists and zoologists classify natural specimens – by identifying common features and subdividing. The activity could have been carried out without the use of a computer, but the branching database imposed a discipline on the children's thinking which might not have otherwise been there (see Turner *et al.*, 1984 and Underwood & Underwood, 1990).

Graphing programs and databases can assist with the analysis of experiments, particularly if patterns in the data are being sought, such as when the children are trying to decide whether there is a consistent relationship between the number of turns of the key for a wind-up car and the distance it travels. Putting the results into a graph-drawing program and plotting a line graph would reveal whether the relationship was consistent through the "straightness" of the line it produced. Expecting infant children to accurately construct a line graph might prove time-consuming, whereas the computer will plot it instantaneously, placing the emphasis more on interpretation than on graph drawing.

Using IT to present findings

Children need to be given opportunities to communicate their scientific work to a wider audience. Factual report writing, making sure the information is accurate and informative, is a skill which takes time and experience to acquire. Some adults have difficulty in focusing on the key issues and communicating factual information concisely. Many word processors are able to include picture images and most graph-drawing programs and databases or

After gathering autumn leaves, the 6-years-olds had to sort them according to their own criteria. The teacher told them first to find a way of dividing the collected leaves into two piles. Mena suggested the brown leaves could be separated from the yellow leaves. Each of the new piles was to be divided again. James suggested "Pointy" leaves and "Not pointy" leaves. Emma suggested "Big" and "Little" leaves as the next category. Their teacher asked them to decide which of the middle-sized leaves was big and which was little. James suggested they measured them and any that were longer than 5 cm were big, any that were less than 5 cm were little. And so the sorting continued. Once the children had sorted the leaves physically into 16 different piles, they transferred their ideas to a branching database (*Tree* (SEMERC)). The program asked the children to devise questions to which there were "Yes" or "No" answers. "Is it yellow?" was their first question and "Is it pointed?" was their next, and so on. With their branching key, they could now quickly classify any leaf which was brought into the classroom.

spreadsheets can have their graphs saved as picture files. It is therefore possible for upper Key Stage 1 children to present their findings in word-processed form, complete with graphs.

Counting cars

Rosanna, melissa, Daniel and me went with Mrs Andrews to count cars going past the school gate. We were there for half an hour. We counted 50 cars. White cars were the most. Daniel guessed white cars and he was right. I gessed red cars. We made a graph with Picture point. Mrs Andrews helpd us.

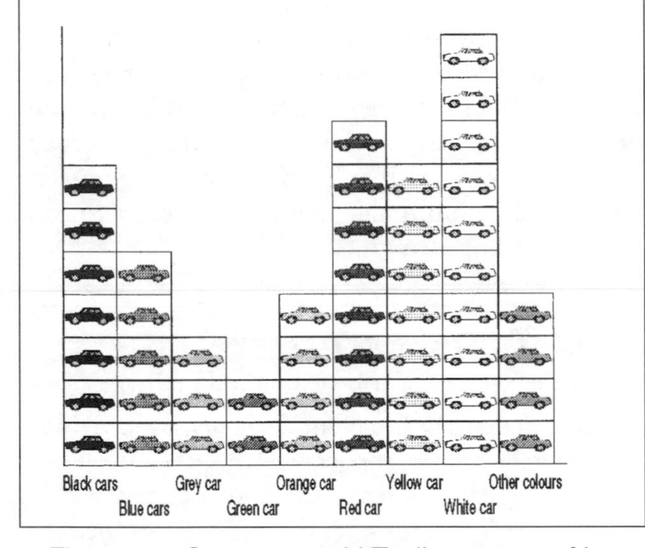

Figure 4.5 Seven-year-old Toni's account of her group's car counting experiment.

IT-based information sources

There is a proliferation of disk- and CD ROM-based information presently on hand for educational use. Much of it is targeted at audiences older than children at Key Stage 1. Some scientific information sources have, however, been written with a younger clientele in mind.

Garden Wildlife (Anglia TV) is available as both disk and CD ROM versions and provides information about the flora and fauna which will be found in most UK gardens. The CD ROM version includes video clips from Anglia TV's Survival programmes and will help children with identification and provide some background information.

Microsoft's *The Magic School Bus* explores the human body and uses animation to help explain the workings of most of the internal systems of the human body. CD ROMs have been produced for young children covering such aspects as Materials, Dinosaurs, Forces and Space. (See Chapter 5 for more information on the use of CD ROM information sources.)

With expensive resources such as CD ROM software, it is essential the teachers have an opportunity to try it out first (see "Finding out about software" at the start of this chapter).

Extending the range of scientific activities through the use of IT

As science work with young children should be firmly rooted in practical experience, the ways in which IT extends the range of activities for science with older children (e.g. through simulations) is inappropriate. One area which is worth considering however, is that of data logging.

Although the use of a computer to directly monitor and record events is not a requirement of the National Curriculum at Key Stage 1, making use of the computer to measure and record environmental conditions can be very useful for developing young children's understanding. *Sensor Box* (Commotion), for example, is a simple-to-use plug-in interface. It can be used to measure heat, light or sound for any period of time. It can be left overnight or for a week to record the changes in temperature and light in the school classroom, or can monitor how noisy the children are being during a quiet reading session! Most educational monitoring programs show line graphs being drawn in "real time" – as the light, temperature or sound level rises, so the line goes up on the graph. Children gain a great deal of pleasure from using the computer in this way. It has considerable potential for monitoring a wide range of children's experiments very accurately or "scientifically".

Summary

In this chapter we have seen how IT can be integrated into most aspects of English and maths work and can augment some of the work in science. The focus has been on communicating information in English, number enhancement in maths and on information handling in both mathematics and science.

It has been shown that, when used carefully, not only can it support existing classroom activities, but it can extend what is achievable. However, the computer's contribution to both children's learning in the core subjects and their IT capability is more significant if children are given opportunities to engage in more challenging IT activities which extend the existing curriculum.

References

Blythe, K. M. (1990) *Children Learning with LOGO*; NCET

Cockcroft, W. H. ((1982) *Mathematics Counts: Report of the Committee of Enquiry into the Teaching of Mathematics in Schools*; HMSO

Harlen, W. (1985) *Teaching and Learning Primary Science*; Paul Chapman Publishing

Liebeck, P. (1984) *How Children Learn Mathematics: A Guide for Parents and Teachers*; Penguin

Medwell, J. (1995) Talking Books for Teaching Reading; *Microscope, Autumn no. 46*, pp. 22–5

Miles, M. (1994, The Somerset Talking Computer Project; in Singleton, C. (ed.) *Computers and Dyslexia*; Dyslexia Computer Resource Centre, University of Hull

Papert, S. (1980) *Mindstorms: Children, Computers and Powerful Ideas*; Harvester Wheatsheaf

Straker, A. (1989) *Children Using Computers*; Blackwell

Turner, I. F., Scullion, L. T. & Whyte, J. (1984) Relationships between Reading Ability and Two Types of Classificatory Ability; *Journal of Research and Reading,* vol. 7, pp. 123-34

Underwood, J. & Underwood, G. (1990) *Computers and Learning: Helping Children Acquire Thinking Skills*; Blackwell

5 IT activities and curriculum: the other foundation subjects

What this chapter is about

This chapter focuses on ways in which IT can be used to support, enhance or extend children's studies in the relevant non-core foundation subjects of the National Curriculum – Design and Technology, History and Geography, Art, and Music – and also Religious Education.

In addition, aspects of IT which are covered in this chapter include:

- CD ROM and information retrieval
- The Internet as an information source
- The use of graphics programs
- How sound and music packages can be used

Base 8, the Year 1 class in a new town primary school, centred their half-term's work around the story of the three little pigs. To enhance their work, the teacher used *Three Little Pigs at Home* (Sherston). This simple adventure program runs on a BBC B with a concept keyboard to ease the entering of text. The children's related D&T work introduced them to various techniques for constructing structures by making houses from straw (Artstraws, dried grass stems, spaghetti), sticks (twigs, stripwood, balsa wood) and bricks (Lego, miniature bricks and glue). The children then went on to decide which of the houses would be the strongest. They extended their studies by carrying out a survey of a street in the original village around which their community had grown – making a classroom display of drawings of the buildings and including some descriptive writing.

IT and Design and Technology

Probably the area of the curriculum which causes teachers of primary children the greatest concern (apart from IT) is Design and Technology (D&T). In 1995 only 14% of primary teachers had had 2 or more days' training in D&T (DATA, 1995) so it is hardly surprising that teachers find D&T more difficult than other areas of the curriculum.

Supporting and enhancing D&T activities with IT

Using IT as a starting point

Most simple adventure programs can spawn cross-curricular activities. Ablac, for example, have disk-based talking books for PC computers centred around many of the well-known fairy tales which can be used as starting points for D&T and other activities such as:

- making scaled-up items such as a cup or a pair of spectacles for the giant in *Jack and the Beanstalk*;
- designing a humane wolf-trap for *Little Red Riding Hood*;
- building bridges for the Little and Medium-sized *Billy Goats Gruff*;
- making stronger furniture for Baby Bear in *Goldilocks*.

Many programs featuring teddy bears can similarly form the basis for D&T activities – making clothes for Teddy, making furniture for Teddy's home or a bed or wheelchair when Teddy is ill. The Freddy Teddy Playground program (Topologika) provides an invaluable introduction to LOGO programming, which is the basis for most computer control languages (see Chapter 4, "Mathematics and IT", and below).

Market testing with IT

These days, products are rarely introduced without extensive market testing to predict the likely extent of consumer interest. On a smaller scale, Key Stage 1 children might need to survey the preferences of their classmates for the most popular food items in a picnic, or the design of packaging for a new soft drink they had devised.

The infant department of one primary school decided to organise a picnic as part of their annual outing. One group of Year 2 children was given the responsibility of finding out which items would be most popular and how many children would be likely to eat them, and to indicate how much food ought to be bought. They devised a questionnaire using *Junior Pinpoint* (Longman Logotron) on which all the information was entered. To save time, all the children in the school were interviewed individually and their responses entered straight into the computer.

Once all the data were entered, the "researchers" were able to accurately inform the teachers as to how many children would be likely to eat cheese spread rolls on brown bread, how many preferred orange juice to milk and whether apples would go down better than bananas.

Designing and IT

As part of their shopping topic, one group of Year 1/Year 2 children designed packaging for soft drinks. A computer painting package enabled them to experiment with different colours for prominent features on their packaging. They decided that blues and greens made them think of cool drinks, whereas reds, yellows and oranges colours made them think of flavours. Their collection of drinks cartons from the local supermarket suggested orange and red were the most common colours used for drinks packaging.

Some paint packages (e.g. *Dazzle!* (SEMERC)) allow the children to experiment with different coloured backgrounds or change the "filled" colour for a region. In this way, the children are able to experiment with different colour combinations for their packaging designs or try different colour schemes for Teddy's house. Incidentally, an "UNDO" option is essential for this type of activity – so that the original colour can be restored if the picture is spoiled.

Computer aided design

Designers and older secondary children make use of computer aided design (CAD) programs to assist with their designing process. Similar packages are used by some companies for working out the layout of kitchen units or the most appropriate design for a conservatory using pre-assembled units. For Key Stage 1 children, there are files for *My World 2* (SEMERC) which help children design their own castle, wrist watch, sandwich or pizza, town or village, garden, kitchen or any other room in a house. All the files follow the familiar *My World* point-and-drag feature and some include print-outs which can be cut out and used as nets for card models.

A more ambitious CAD package, specifically for use by Key Stage 2 children and older infants, is available (*KidCAD* (Ablac)) which enables children to view their designs from various angles. A house, for example, could be drawn as a three-dimensional isometric view then shown in plan or front view. *Home Mapper* (TAG), a generalised package for use with a "Homes" topic, includes activities for supporting house and room designing.

Using IT for communicating D&T

A word-processed document can be used by children to record their D&T experiences, but is this the most imaginative and challenging use of IT? What is the purpose of the activity, if the teacher already knows what has happened?

The teacher of one Year 2 class overcomes the somewhat contrived task of asking children to write about their D&T activities by keeping a "design portfolio". This is a classroom resource for all children to refer to for ideas for their own designing and making. Making use of IT means the children can print out one copy for the class portfolio, one copy for themselves and, if required, one for the child's assessment file.

We have seen how clip-art pictures can be incorporated into children's work but IT can be used to extend the ways in which children can communicate information about their designing and making.

Extending D&T activities through the use of IT

Communicating through IT

A purposeful activity which combines text with images is the creation of advertising leaflets bestowing the virtues of the children's designed products.

Figure 5.1 An advertising flyer made by Year 2 children to advertise their puppets

The children who produced this advertising flyer had had very little experience of IT other than some simple word processing. The photograph of the puppet was taken by a digital camera. The image from the camera was then transferred to the computer (by connecting a lead from the camera to the computer). Once in the computer, the image was then re-sized and pasted into a drawing program (*Claris Works*) so the text could be added.

Digital cameras are not cheap, at around £300. They can be loaned from local authority or higher education institutions (as in the above instance); clusters of schools have been known to pool their resources to share such equipment. A far more cost-effective approach for schools which already have a CD ROM drive is to have conventional photographs "developed" as a photo CD. This can be done at a leading high street chemists or by photo-developing specialists. The cost is slightly more than for normal processing but once the digitised images are placed on the CD ROM, they can be readily transferred into many word-processor or graphics packages.

A less technological approach to this activity is for the text to be written on the computer and for the child to draw the image directly on the poster once it has been printed out.

Computer control

Using programmable floor turtles such as Roamer (*Valiant*) and Pip (*Swallow*) has become an accepted activity for most infant schools and departments. By typing in a series of instructions, the robot can be made to negotiate a maze, deliver letters to houses in a "pretend" street, explore a magic garden or perform a dance or gymnastic sequence.

Teaching the robot to follow a sequence of instructions, evaluating the turtle's actions and "de-bugging" mistakes are the basics of computer control.

Once the children have mastered the programming of a floor turtle, the natural progression is for them to program a screen turtle. *First LOGO* (Longman Logotron) provides a relatively painless introduction to LOGO programming, though older Key Stage 1 children can use a full version of LOGO, provided the activities are structured to sustain their interest.

The teacher of one Year 2 class decided to introduce the children to LOGO through her "Journeys" theme. She prepared a LOGO program in which various "planets" were drawn on the screen. The children had then to guide a rocket-shaped turtle from planet to planet by typing in LOGO commands.

For more information about LOGO, refer to Chapter 4, "Mathematics and IT".

IT and History and Geography

In the infant school, history and geography are often taught together under integrated topics centred on the local environment. Much of the information handling which underpins work in these subjects is similar, as are some of the skills.

First-hand experience and secondary sources of information

Much of the work in history and geography at Key Stage 1 is enquiry-based. Teachers want the children to act as historians or geographers, gathering information, making connections, forming hypotheses and theories, and testing their ideas in the field. The majority of the children's work should be experiential – making use of their immediate and local environments. IT has a part to play in this process, provided it is used sensitively.

There comes a time, however, when information needs to be garnered from secondary sources. Since the introduction of CD ROMs, multimedia encyclopaedias and reference material has burgeoned. The Internet has made information more accessible and immediate than ever before. So where and how should an infant school or department with limited resources make best use of these new technologies to assist with the teaching and learning of history and geography?

Supporting and enhancing the teaching and learning of History and Geography with IT

Creating information

As has already been stated, there is no substitute for direct experience, but IT-based data handling can help focus the children's attention on significant details and sharpen their enquiry skills.

As part of a study of their locality, the Year 2 class in one primary school carried out a survey of their parents' opinions about the shopping area. They wanted to find out what sort of things they bought, how often they used the area, and whether there were any additional facilities which they would like made available.

The problem with surveys of this kind is often, what do we do with the information once we have gathered it? What does it tell us? What's it for? In this case, the children used the findings of this initial survey to carry out a more focused subsequent enquiry. They found, for example, that one parent suggested a bookshop might be useful. Was this the only person who wanted it, or had other people just not thought of it? Several others suggested a swimming pool might prove popular – but would other users of the shopping area agree? What about elderly residents – would they have other needs?

The children decided they needed more information. They conducted another survey of actual users of the shopping area by interviewing them (with an adult "assistant").

This time, they noted down the approximate age of the person (young, middle-aged or old), their gender, and where they lived. They also asked questions about specific facilities (library, bookshop, swimming pool), as well as asking for further ideas. Their analysis of these data was far more focused – would older people be more likely to prefer a library and would younger people prefer a swimming pool? Did more older people than younger people use the shops? The computer database (*Junior Pinpoint* (Longman Logotron)) enabled the children to select particular groups of people (the middle-aged, those who wanted a library, those who lived on the local estate) and draw pie charts of their preferences so that comparisons could be made.

The teacher did not use a computer for the first survey. It wasn't needed. The information could be readily interpreted without the need for IT. The second survey was greatly assisted by the use of IT. The quantity of data and the complexity of the enquiries meant that IT was more than useful – it was almost essential. The children gained valuable experience through both activities. The first survey helped them understand the process of data gathering so that when they came to use the computer for their second survey, they already understood what was happening. Carrying out a preliminary "real" data handling exercise is seen as an important precursor to working on the computer (see Gifford & Pepperell, 1992).

Using information sources

> A few years ago I would never have thought that infants were capable of doing the sort of work on information skills which I have seen them do from the age of 4 onwards. (Davies, 1985, p. 26)

As with most enquiry-led work, the nature and purpose of the enquiry is a key factor. If children want to find out what a Victorian child wore, copying a picture is far more useful than writing out a piece of text. Finding out when a local historical house was built, and by whom, will require a single date or name to complete a half-composed sentence. Trying to find out what it was like to live in the house in Victorian times will require considerably more reading and comprehension. The greatest strength of IT lies in its ability to store, present and manipulate information. The skills children need to access information from IT sources is different from, but no less important than, those required for researching book-based information.

CD ROM encyclopaedias

Gathering information from IT-based sources, such as CD ROM encyclopaedias, places more emphasis on the interpretation and synthesis of the information than on the skills required to locate it. CD ROMs, particularly those aimed at younger children, usually include a number of different routes to finding the information of which alphabetically arranged indexes are only one option. In many cases, the children simply type in a key word and the computer will show the "pages" which include this reference. Other CD ROMs allow the children to "browse" through the information and gradually home in on that which is required.

Once the information has been located, many CD ROM packages allow the user to print the information (pictures, too) and save it as a file on a separate disk to be imported into a word processor or desktop publishing package.

If text and pictures are extracted and "pasted" directly into the children's own work, then the development of skills in selecting and reconstructing information is even more desirable. This places emphasis on the teacher organising activities which help develop IT-based enquiry skills to help avoid children copying meaningless "chunks" of information verbatim. To overcome this difficulty, there are some strategies for making the best use of CD ROM based information.

1. Ensure the children's enquiries are quite specific so that snippets of information are all they need to discover. These can then be "noted" down for incorporation in the children's own narrative accounts.
2. Develop the children's note-taking skills so that only important facts are written down (see Davies, 1985).
3. Allow the children to extract text and place it in a word processor, but insist that it is then thoroughly edited.
4. Allow the children only to export pictures, and insist they must devise their own captions to accompany them.

At this juncture (mid-1997), there are several CD ROM and floppy-disk-based information packages which are specifically aimed at young users (See Table 5.4). This list will be outdated almost as soon as it is written, but does provide some indication as to what is available. It is advisable, however, to consult up-to-date catalogues and software directories to find out what has been produced more recently, as CD ROMs are currently being published at a phenomenal rate.

Title	Supplier	Type	Computer
My First Encylopaedia	Guildsoft	CD ROM	PC
Random House Kids Encylopaedia CD ROM	Guildsoft	CD ROM	Acorn or PC
Grolier Guinness Disc of Records	Mindscope	CD ROM	PC
Photobase (various history topics in pictures)	Longman Logotron	CD ROM	Acorn or PC
The Discoverers (early technology today)	Guildsoft	CD ROM	PC
Castles	Anglia TV	CD ROM	All
Explorapedia – The World of People	Microsoft	CD ROM	PC Windows
My First World Atlas	Impressions	Floppy	PC or Apple
Oxford Talking Infant Atlas	Sherston	Floppy	PC

Table 5.4 CD ROM encyclopaedias

Presenting historical and geographical information with IT

We have already seen how IT can be used to communicate information in textual and/or in image form. As has been mentioned, clip-art and photo files exist for practically every area of the curriculum, enabling children to insert pictures into their word-processed documents. But there is no need to stop there. If children are gaining experience with seeking information presented in multimedia form on CD ROM, why not produce their own interactive multimedia packages?

Extending activities in History and Geography through IT

Multimedia

Stephen Heppell (1994) suggests that multimedia encourages us to move away from the deficiency model of the learner (empty vessels waiting to be filled) to one that recognises the learner's emergent capabilities: "Real change is likely to occur not by trying exclusively to deliver old learning outcomes with new technology, but by looking for new learning outcomes that can only be delivered by that technology" (p. 158).

If you feel that creating multimedia presentations is beyond the scope of infant children, then scrutinise some of the entries for the National Educational Multimedia Awards (NEMA). This is an annual competition which has been run by the National Council for Educational Technology (NCET) since 1994. There are seven categories for entry, including one for the under-sevens. Recent winners in the under-sevens category have included:

- *Bones* – an entertaining and informative presentation about the human body (Northgate Primary School, Bishops Stortford)
- *I Hate School!* – a beautifully illustrated story about a child's day at school (Inverkeithing Primary School)
- *The Grumpy Spider* – a lovely illustrated story with interactive sections (Rowdown Infant School, Croydon)
- *Going Wild with Animals* – an information package about animals (Queensbridge Infant School, London E8)

A multimedia authoring package allows children to create various screens of information which can be interlinked by "buttons". When the mouse pointer is moved over the button and the mouse button clicked,

Figure 5.2 A winning entry in the entry in the competition run by the National Council for Educational Technology

something happens: a sound effect is created, part of the screen changes or animates, or the user is taken to a new screen of information. The information on each screen can take the form of text, pictures, photos, sounds, moving images, or any combination of these. Authoring packages which are suitable for use by Key Stage 1 children include *Hyperstudio* (TAG) and *Ultima* (SEMERC). With these packages, children and teachers can create their own talking books or multimedia information presentations.

Importing images and sounds into the computer
Graphic images can be created by the children or taken from a clip-art library and pasted on to a page. Images can be drawn on paper and scanned into the computer with hand-held or flat-bed scanners. Digital cameras can send images directly to the computer or put on a photo CD (see above) and images from a video camera or recorder can be frozen and imported into the computer. Sounds, including the children's own voices, can be incorporated into the pages and, of course, text can be typed in. Although much of this sounds technical and complicated, even the most technophobic teachers and students find it is far less daunting than they thought, once they have overcome the initial "I could never do that" hurdle.

Once all the pages have been designed and constructed, they are linked together to create an information package about any relevant topic – the school, the local community, a visit, animals, etc. As with any activity of this kind, the process which is gone through in the planning, gathering, re-working and presentation of the information is as important, if not more so, than the end result.

The intended audience for such a project will determine the type of information which is being presented and the way in which it is portrayed. One way of extending the audience for one's work is to place it on the Internet.

The Internet

According to the major political parties, by the time this book is published practically every school will be linked to the information superhighway. That remains to be seen, but the World Wide Web is already being used by a number of first schools. Imagine having access to a database which stores information on virtually every major computer in the world – that is the potential of the Internet. Imagine being able to communicate with practically any other computer in the world at the click of a mouse button – that is the reality of the World Wide Web: "it has turned out that the last 200 feet, the distance from the school office to the teacher's classroom, is the most difficult to traverse electronically. Classroom teachers remain the only professionals in the world without convenient and easy access to telephones" (Wolpert & Lowney, 1991).

Already there are Internet providers which cater specifically for schools' and educational use – BT Campus World (British Telecom), Internet for Learning (Research Machines), The Education Exchange (Edex) and others which cater for educational establishments, BBC Networking Club, Compuserve, Cix, Demon and Pipex.

To link up to the Internet, all that is needed is a computer with a hard drive, a modem and a piece of communications software (usually provided free of charge when you subscribe). Subscription rates are around £10 per month plus the cost of the phone calls – usually charged at the local rate.

Access to the Internet provides:

- Information, through "visiting" web sites run by schools, universities, museums, art galleries, organisations such as NASA or Greenpeace, companies, libraries and individuals. Children can search for information and teachers can download ideas and even classroom resource material.
- Electronic mail (e-mail), by which information and enquiries can be received or sent to any other user of the Internet – including the President of the USA.
- Access to discussion groups – there is a group devoted to UK teachers (an electronic staffroom) to exchange information, opinions and ideas.
- Guaranteed opportunities to publish your own material worldwide on the network – free of charge (apart from the subscription).

When the infant children at one primary school were studying St Lucia as part of their Geography work, the Year 2 children were able to "visit" the country, see pictures of various locations and interview one of its leading inhabitants via the Internet.

Some of the information for this book has come through e-mail communication with colleagues, schools and educational organisations. Without moving from the computer, the writer has been able to contact teachers, search through library catalogues, check references, and seek articles in universities in most parts of the world.

There is insufficient space in this chapter to do more than touch upon the opportunities which the Internet provides. Some suggested reading is included at the end of this chapter for those who want to pursue this aspect further.

Simulations and adventures

There are simulations which enable young children to gain some experience of life in the past or in exploring other environments. *Richard Scarry's Busy Town* (Paramount Interactive) is an example of a simulation devised for younger users. The program allows children to explore a town and help its inhabitants with various tasks. Although based on an imaginary town, it could be used to augment children's local studies. *Zoopak* (4mation) provides a selection of computer-based activities and support material centred on zoos.

It should be borne in mind that at Key Stage 1, a simulation is no real substitute for direct experience and an imaginative teacher.

IT and Art

Since the introduction of computers which use a mouse, computer painting and drawing activities have become commonplace in the infant classroom. Apart from providing first-class practice in mouse manipulation, these programs provide a means for children to make use of the computer's other great feature beyond the manipulation of text and numbers – the production of visual images. Queries may arise as to what contribution the computer can play in the development of children's artistic skills and knowledge if: "Art education ... involves developing the senses through looking, touching, listening, smelling and even tasting" (Pluckrose, 1984).

However: "The computer is a wonderfully versatile and effective medium for art. Computers aid drawing and design by allowing images to be easily moved, repeated or enlarged and any mistakes can be easily erased without loss of face" (Mathieson, 1993, p. 34).

This section explores the implications of the above statement in more detail.

Supporting and enhancing Art activities with IT

The computer has several advantages over traditional art materials and equipment, in that computer-based artwork:

- is not messy;
- allows unlimited experimentation without the wasting of materials;
- allows for easy and flexible pattern making;
- permits different stages in the process of creating an image to be saved and/or printed;
- supports controllable colour mixing and blending (with some paint packages);
- allows mistakes to be easily rectified or modified;
- enables other people's pictures to be used, modified or edited.

There are of course, obvious disadvantages:

- the computer provides only secondary experience which cannot match the manipulation of actual materials, tools and equipment;
- mouse control is more difficult than the use of conventional tools;
- colour printing is expensive and can yield disappointing results;
- the final image is usually restricted in size to a maximum of A4.

If the computer is regarded as just another medium or tool which can be drawn upon for visually representing the world around us, then computer-based artwork is seen in its proper perspective.

This computerised picture was produced by 7-year-old Polly as her response to one of Monet's sunflower pictures. Other children in her class used more conventional art materials for their response.

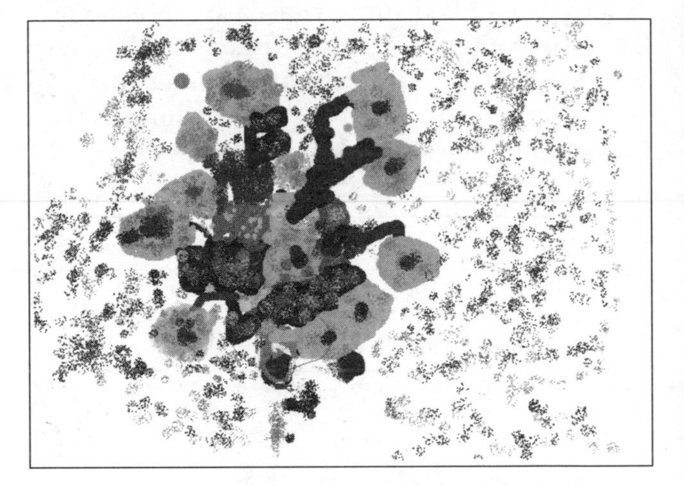

Figure 5.3 Polly's Monet

Some of the effects which graphics packages replicate would be difficult to achieve in the infant classroom without the use of the computer. Polly has used a computerised airbrush to create some of her misty impressionist effects and yet its real-life equivalent is not commonly be found in the art cupboard of most infant classrooms.

There is a baffling range of graphics software provided for classroom use, each claiming to be more versatile and appropriate than the rest. Apart from software which has been written for specific purposes such as tiling or pattern making (see below), computer-based graphics packages tend to fall into one of two categories: painting or drawing.

The difference between drawing and painting on the computer

A painting package

When a mark is made on the screen with a tool in a painting package, the mark remains fixed – as paint would be fixed to a piece of paper. Painting packages vary as to the tools they provide. The simplest package will provide little more than a "brush" which might be variable in shape or size. The most sophisticated packages include tools for drawing shapes and for performing effects on areas of the picture – copying, moving, flipping, reflecting, blurring, outlining, posterising and so on.

The advantage of a painting package is its ease of use with young children and the way it models "real" painting. The disadvantage is the lack of editing flexibility once a mark has been made on the screen.

A drawing package

A drawing package identifies each shape drawn as a separately defined element. These elements, once drawn, can be individually highlighted and moved, resized, reshaped, refilled with colour, and have many other effects applied to them, dependent upon the level of sophistication of the package.

The advantage of a drawing package is the flexibility it provides in editing pictures. The disadvantage is that they can be fiddly for young children to use.

Just as some children prefer using pencil crayons while others favour paints or felt tips, some IT packages are more appropriate to the creative and temperamental attributes of some children than others. More importantly, different IT art packages are better suited to some tasks than others. As children progress through their primary schooling, they need to gain experience with both drawing and painting programs to be in a position to make

As part of their topic on water, the children in one mixed Reception/Year 1 class practised their IT skills by creating pictures of fish with a painting program (*Easy Works* with *Claris Works* (Claris)). Six-year-old Julia's fish was painstakingly painted as an outline and filled with a graduated pattern selected from the palette.

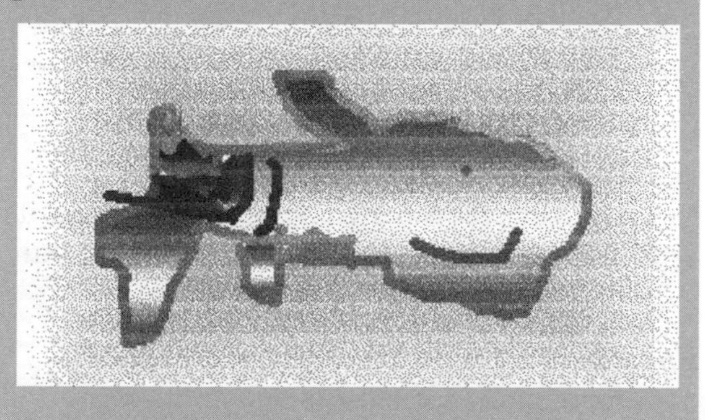

Figure 5.4 Julia's fish painting

Five-year-old James is noted for his meticulousness. Growing increasingly frustrated in trying to control the on-screen paint brush with the mouse, the teacher realised he might find a drawing package more manageable. She showed him how to overlap different filled shapes to produce an irregular outline. After a little experimentation, James was very pleased with his fish.

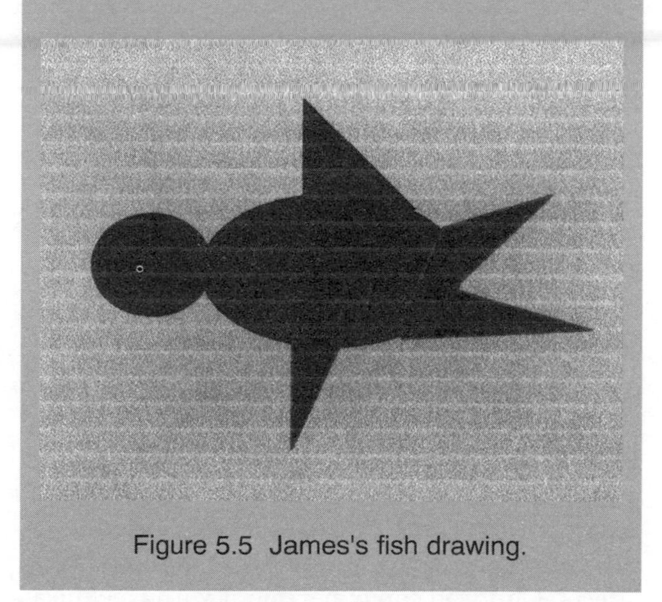

Figure 5.5 James's fish drawing.

informed choices as to which type of software might be most appropriate for certain tasks. Although not a hard and fast rule, painting packages tend to be better suited for more spontaneous and creative artistic activities, whereas drawing packages tend to be better suited to the creation of images which require a certain degree of precision.

Figure 5.6 Four-year-old Amy's first experiments with mark making on the computer

What to look for in computer-based art packages

When choosing a graphics software package, the following features may help determine its appropriateness for the children's skill, experience or developmental levels.

Entry level
- Simple paint tools (brushes of different sizes and shapes, eraser)
- A limited palette of 8–16 colours

Basic level
- Basic tools (brush, pencil, fill)
- Palette of colours and tints (16–32)
- Simple fill patterns/hatching
- An UNDO facility (to undo the last action)

Intermediate level
- A wider range of tools (text tool, airbrush)
- A mixable palette or wide range of colours (256+)
- Cutting, copying and pasting facilities

Advanced level
- More extended tools (e.g. smudge, reflect, stamp, solarisation)
- A zoom facility for fine detailed working

Graphics software for younger children

Graphics packages for the computer vary widely in the options and features they provide. For the youngest children there are very simple painting packages (e.g. *Splosh* (Kudlian) or *Tiny Draw* (Topologika)) which provide a carefully selected range of tools and painting effects. Children can experiment with thickness of line and, with some packages, mix their own colours (e.g. *First Paint* (Resource)).

Some graphics packages offer more features but allow the teacher to tailor them to the level of experience of the children. These packages (e.g. *Dazzle!* (SEMERC), *Colour Magic* (RM)) allow the children to be offered increasingly more demanding tools and techniques as they develop in skill and confidence without the need for them to learn how to use a completely new package.

Patterning and tiling

Patterning is a strength of computer-based graphics. Many full-featured graphics packages allow the children to paint or fill sections of their pictures with shading, cross-hatching or patterning. Some of the more sophisticated graphics software (e.g. *Revelation* (Longman Logotron) and *Kid Pix* (ESM)) allow images or "motifs" to be repeatedly "stamped" over the screen to create patterns.

Some tiling programs, such as *Tessellations* for *My World 2* (SEMERC), *Mosaic* (SEMERC) or *Versatile* (Oak Solutions), are specifically written to allow children to experiment with and create tiled or tessellated patterns. Patterns involving lines or shapes can form the basis or inspiration for replication in other media such as string pictures, press prints, block/object printing, relief printing or simple screen printing.

Ideas for computer art

As we have already seen, computer-based art packages can be used as the inspiration for artwork such as pattern making, or the work of other artists or the environment can inspire computerised art work. Below are some ideas which are appropriate for young children.

- Turning "mouse" scribbles into pictures (introduces the idea of editing)
- Reflecting and rotating scribbles to make patterns
- Creating pictures with blobs of colour (gross Pointillism?)
- Representing a scene with a series of coloured shapes (Cubism?)
- Drawing a scene with only the airbrush (Impressionism?)
- Restricting the palette to only shades and tints of one colour
- Drawing a chair with the mouse, without looking at the screen (or even turning the monitor off)
- Reproducing parts of great works
- Drawing on the screen with a water-based marker pen and "tracing" behind it with the mouse
- As above, but drawing on an overhead projector transparency sheet and placing this over the screen
- Making press prints or string pictures based on print-outs
- Tracing computerised images with fabric crayons and then ironing these on to tee-shirts or drapes
- Making greetings cards by combining pictures with text
- Adding patterned borders to pieces of poetry or pages of text

Kevin Mathieson's (1993) *Children's Art and the Computer* provides more ideas and shares in some of the author's experiences of using computers for artwork with very young children.

Art appreciation and the computer

The National Curriculum reminds us that we should provide children with opportunities to study the works of well-known artists. Some CD ROMs and sites on the Internet enable children to examine great works of art in close detail – in some cases, under the guidance of a narrator or informed commentator. Sections of these could be used selectively to enhance or support work which was being carried out in the classroom using other stimuli such as prints or illustrations.

Extending art activities through the use of the computer

Clip-art

As has been mentioned previously, clip-art files are available for all computers covering a wide range of topics. These are available in either CD ROM or floppy-disk format. Clip-art images can be pasted directly into most word processors or can be imported into graphics packages to be edited. At the simplest level, editing can be little more than resizing or reshaping the image. For the more adventurous, clip-art images can be edited more substantially.

Figure 5.7 Anneka (aged 7) removed the rider from this horse

To make fine-detailed changes such as the one shown in figure 5.7, the graphics package needs a zoom facility. All computer images (including text) are comprised of a series of small dots called *pixels*. For children (and teachers) who are blessed with patience, zooming in on areas of a picture enable fine-detailed drawing or changes to carried out. Even quite young Key Stage 1 children have little difficulty appreciating the relationship between the enlarged section of the image and its full-sized version.

Scanning and digitising

In the previous section, we saw how children's photographs can be imported into the computer. Through the use of a scanner, children's drawings can similarly be transferred into the computer. In most cases, a black-and-white scanner would be sufficient – as colour scanners cost considerably more and use large amounts of computer memory. The process of scanning is not too difficult and is well within the capabilities of most 6- or 7-year-olds. Being able to scan in an image they have drawn not only develops the children's knowledge and understanding of IT devices, it enables children who have problems or frustrations when drawing with a mouse to place their art work into the computer. A scanner also enables illustrations from books or leaflets to be imported into the computer for inclusion in the children's IT work – or to be used as the basis for their own artwork.

Learning about IT through computerised artwork

As we have seen, not only does computer-based artwork provide an opportunity for young children to practise and develop their manipulative skills with the mouse, it can introduce them to:

- how images can be edited with a computer;
- how graphic images can be combined with text (introducing desktop publishing);
- computerised techniques and effects;
- the way the screen displays images as a series of dots or pixels;
- input devices such as scanners.

IT and Music

"You do not have to be a musician to be musical". (Dankworth, 1984)

People who recall the music produced by the early home computers will recall its tinny beep. Computers have moved on considerably since those early days, thanks mainly to the vast increases in computer memories and the speed with which they can now handle complex information. Even quite basic computer-based music software is capable of reproducing creditable synthesised sounds.

The music curriculum stipulates that children should be provided with opportunities to participate in music making with their own bodies (through singing, clapping, stamping and banging) and through the use of percussive and tuned instruments – some of which could be of their own making.

Supporting and enhancing music activities with IT

For teachers who are not confident musicians, making music can be somewhat daunting, particularly if some of the children are already receiving additional music tuition. Musical composition and notation is generally left to teachers with specialist skills and knowledge. This arrangement is not always convenient or possible in some schools. Although IT is no panacea, some music software enables children to compose their own original pieces of melodious music with minimal musical knowledge. Furthermore, such software provides useful experience for children in moving from idiosyncratic pictorial representation of music to the more conventional staff notation.

With *Beetles* (Brilliant Computing), the children can "give" beetle musicians different instruments and hear tunes being played with their choice of accompaniment – does a lullaby sound better with violins or with a trumpet? As the program is entirely graphically based, it is suited to quite young children. There are options which enable the teacher to configure it for use with nursery children.

Compose World (Expressive Software) is an imaginative piece of software which presents children with pictorial symbols or words, each of which represents a phrase of music. By arranging the symbols in sequences of their own choosing, children produce a harmonious melody – no matter how the phrases are ordered. The phrases and their representative symbols can be edited by the teacher and there are files of phrases to fit different themes (spooky, Eastern, Baroque, jaunty and so on).

Music Box (Topologika), for example, presents children with a screen of horizontal bars on which symbols can be placed; the nearer the top of the screen the symbol is placed, the higher the note. By positioning a series of symbols on the bars, a tune is composed.

Various programs (e.g. *Notate* (Longman Logotron)) present children with a musical staff on which conventional notes can be positioned to be played back. For children who are well advanced with music, these pieces of software provide a number of options. In some cases, it is possible for an electronic keyboard with MIDI output to be connected to the computer and for the notes on the computer screen to be played automatically by the keyboard – a modern-day pianola! These programs usually include an option which allows information to flow in the opposite direction – from keyboard to computer. A tune picked out on the keyboard is automatically written on the staff – ideal for budding composers!

Extending music activities through the use of IT

Musical appreciation and CD ROM

No matter what your musical taste, there is now likely to be a CD ROM package which will enable you to explore the genre and steer you through its complexities. For young children, there are CD ROMs which present information about musical instruments (e.g. *Musical Instruments* (Microsoft)) and cover most of the principal classical composers (e.g. *Music Series* (Microsoft)). *Tuneland* (Longman Logotron) is geared more specifically towards a younger audience and provides a whole range of activities based on familiar children's songs. *Peter and the Wolf* (TDC Interactive) makes use of the multimedia environment to enable children to interactively engage with this well-known introduction to classical music.

For those without sophisticated hardware, there are still some very useful computer-based activities available for the trusty BBC B computer. *Compose* (Expressive Software) is the BBC B originator of *Compose World* (Expressive Software). *Peter Beater's Music Games* (System Applied Technology) and *Music Maker* (Resource) include a number of activities which practise aural skills such as pitch recognition and an appreciation of note length.

Multimedia, sound effects and Music

The multimedia authoring package *Hyperstudio* (TAG) is provided with a file of sounds and music which the children can use simply by selecting them from a menu. Lisa, Laura, Preety and Dionne's adventure story was their first venture into multimedia with *Hyperstudio*. They soon discovered how to add a piece of music or a sound effect whenever a new page was shown. They spent some time discussing which sort of sound ought to introduce each page. They decided to compose some of their own music for the next adventure they write.

The inexpensive *Ultima* (SEMERC) and more advanced packages such as *Genesis Project* (Oak Solutions) and *Magpie* (Longman Logotron) include a small range of sound effects. In the same way as there are clip-art files of pictures which can be included with children's word processing, there are also clip-files of music and sound effects which can be "pasted" into multimedia presentations (e.g. *Grooves* (MDI)). The ease with which this can be achieved varies with each multimedia package and to some extent is dependent upon the type of computer on which you are working. At the time of writing, *Hyperstudio* (TAG) provides the most straightforward approach to the incorporation of sound and music with text and pictures.

Programmable turtles, LOGO and Music

LOGO programming is associated principally with turtle graphics or the programmed movement of a robot. The Roamer (Valiant) and Pip turtles (Swallow), and most versions of LOGO, include commands for creating simple tunes. Just as the turtle can be programmed to carry out a series of movements, it can similarly be programmed to play a series of notes.

With many versions of LOGO and with Pip, the instructions required are simply a letter signifying the note, followed by a number indicating the duration of the note. For example, E 2 D 2 C 4 E 2 D 2 C 4 would play the beginning of *Three Blind Mice*.

Learning about IT with and through Music

Apart from the obvious benefit of developing children's understanding of the computer's ability to represent sounds, music activities on the computer provide opportunities to develop other IT knowledge and understanding:

- that information about sounds can be stored and manipulated on a computer in the same way as words and pictures;
- that a piece of music and a computer program are very similar – they are a series of instructions in symbolic form.

IT and Religious Education

The relationship between IT and RE is likely to be tenuous, particularly when considering the spiritual and moral dimension. IT can, of course, be used as an information source for RE, just as it can for other subjects of the curriculum.

Supporting and enhancing RE activities with IT

IT can be used to enhance work in many of the familiar infant topics and themes providing opportunities for children to develop IT skills while engaged in RE-related activities. These examples give a flavour of some ways in which IT can be integrated into RE work.

Self and others

Many Key Stage 1 teachers incorporate elements of spiritual and moral education into their topics about the children themselves – "Ourselves" and "All about Me" being two familiar examples.

IT support for this type of activity is well provided for. The *My World* series (SEMERC), for example, includes files entitled "Me" and "I'm Special" which encourage the children to gather and compare information about themselves and each other. *All about Me* (Northern Micromedia) uses very simple text entry to enable Reception children to create a booklet about themselves.

Festivals and celebrations

A familiar classroom activity in many primary schools is the study of festivals, the implication being that by finding out about important religious events and their significance, some insight is gained into what a religion values and how it works.

Making greeting cards is an activity which tends to be associated with such studies. Some educational word processors (e.g. *Full Phase* (SEMERC) provide templates for the making of greeting cards, while *MakeIT* (Soft Teach) is a program which is specifically designed to enable children to incorporate computerised pictures into a greeting card format.

There are clip-art files of pictures associated with many religious festivals (e.g. *Christmas Artwork* (SPA), *Ethnic Borders* (4mation), RE *Themes and Topics* (Cleveland ECC)) which can be used as sources for children's cards. The children could, alternatively, draw their own designs using a graphics package.

Religious stories

Most of the software which presents religious events is aimed at older children (e.g. *Bible Lands* or *Bible Stories* (Encyclopaedia Britannica)). Some talking stories have a moralistic theme or message, but are not overtly religious. There are clip-art files which depict historical people from other lands which could be incorporated into children's word-processed retelling of religious stories (e.g. *Christmas Allsorts* (Sherston), *Graphics Explosion* (Ablac))

Religious artefacts

The use of religious artefacts to enhance the teaching of comparative religion has grown in recent years. Children are also encouraged to explore designs and patterns of religious significance, such as Celtic, Rangoli and Islamic designs. As many of these are geometrical in origin, computer graphics provide opportunities for children to explore these art forms, making use of the computer's capabilities to draw shapes accurately. LOGO is the most flexible drawing tool for the creation of repeated geometrical patterns and can produce some fascinating designs by, for example, repeating a series of moves several times.

Some of the computer-based tiling programs (see "IT and Art" above) are suitable for creating patterns but tend to be overly complicated for very young children.

Summary – IT across the curriculum

We have seen, in this and the previous chapter, how IT can contribute to or extend activities in all curriculum areas. In this sense, IT can be a unifying factor which binds them together. Creating a multimedia presentation about the school's locality, for example, can bring together a number of subject areas and develop a range of IT skills and knowledge.

These two chapters have provided a series of ideas and starting points for the incorporation of IT into children's subject studies. There are far more ideas and suggestions than would be achievable or desirable. What is important is that children are provided with opportunities to systematically develop their IT skills, knowledge and understanding through carrying out purposeful activities in meaningful contexts. The question a teacher ought to be asking when planning for IT ought to be: "What IT skills and knowledge do the children need to develop next? Are there any opportunities in what I intend to cover in other areas of the curriculum for this to happen?"

It is better for the children and the teacher to use a few pieces of content-free software flexibly and well, than for them to touch upon a wide range of different programs superficially. This aspect will be explored further in the next chapter, when we examine IT in the classroom.

References

Dankworth, A. (1984) Making Music; in Fontana, D. (ed.) *The Education of the Young Child*; Blackwell

DATA (1995) *A Survey of the Capitation Allowances, Resources and INSET Needs for Design and Technology in Primary and Secondary Schools in 1994/5: Research Paper Number Three*; Design and Technology Association

Davies, D. (1985) Introducing Information Skills in the Infant School; in Avann, P. (ed.) *Teaching Information Skills in the Primary School*; Edward Arnold

Gifford, S. & Pepperell, S. (1992) Young Learners use Databases: A Critique of the Mathematical Learning Opportunities; in Lodge, J. (ed.) *Computer Data Handling in the Primary School*; David Fulton in Association with Roehampton Institute

Heppell, S. (1994) Multimedia and Learning: Normal Children, Normal Lives and Real Change; in Underwood, J. (ed.) *Computer Based Learning: Potential into Practice*; David Fulton Publishers

Mathieson, K. (1993) *Children's Art and the Computer*; Hodder and Stoughton

Pluckrose, H. (1984) Learning and Teaching Art and Craft Skills; in Fontana, D. (ed.) *The Education of the Young Child*; Blackwell

Wolpert, E. M. & Lowney, F. A. (1991) Building an Electronic Community; *Educational Technology*, vol. 31 (4), pp. 21– 4

Further reading – the Internet

Mailer, N. & Dickinson, B. (1994) *The UK School Internet Primer*; Koeksuster Publications

Moore, P. (ed.) (1995) *Teaching and Learning with the Internet*; BT Campus World

Meralli, Z., Blamire., R., Brown, M. C. & Kenny, J. (1995) *Highways to Learning: An Introduction to the Internet for Schools and Colleges*; NCET

6 IT in the classroom

What this chapter is about

This chapter examines issues which class teachers need to consider when using computers, covering such areas as:

- the organisation of IT resources;
- the role of the teacher in planning, monitoring, assessing and evaluating IT activities;
- planning for integration of IT into normal classroom activities;
- the teacher as a user of IT.

Managing and organising the classroom and resources for IT

Although many things have a bearing on the successful organisation of the classroom – the building, the children, the resources – the most significant factor is the teacher. She can decide the physical layout of the furniture in the classroom, the grouping and organisation of the children and the way time is utilised. She also has considerable influence over the children's attitudes to their work and the focus of their computer-based activities.

The following organisational systems have been seen in infant classrooms. You might like to consider the advantages and disadvantages of each in relation to your own teaching situation.

An average-sized suburban infant school

Each teaching area has its own computer, though the computers are of varying vintages. The school is gradually acquiring hard-drive-based computers as funds allow. Most classrooms have their computer on a trolley in a designated work space with all the resources to hand. There is a specific scheme of work for Communicating and Handling Information which is integrated with the school's rolling programme of themes.

The children use the computer on a rota basis, a list being posted on the wall in each bay beside the computer. The children use the computer to carry out set tasks which have been allocated by the teacher according to each child's needs, based on the class theme. The teacher records their progress in a class record book and has one very reliable parent helper who assists specifically with IT work for two half-days per week.

The infant department of a 350-pupil primary school

There is one computer in or adjacent to each classroom – now mostly hard-disk-based Acorn machines. IT activities are included in the normal rotational programme of activities. In the space of two weeks, all the children in the class (working in pairs) carry out their IT task for that period. Many of the IT activities are the same for all children, with different pairs responding to the task according to their abilities. In addition, some spelling and number practice programs are tailored to the levels of ability or experience of the children.

Children complete their own log of their IT activities by pasting copies of their work (first and final drafts) in their "IT progress books". The teacher adds her own comments, indicating the date and the amount of help the child received. She also records the skills each child may next need to acquire to remind herself and to inform others.

The infant class of a small rural school

The class is vertically grouped with all infant ages. There are two computers, an old BBC B and a more recent hard-disk-based PC. Both computers and a fax machine are situated in the IT corner, partially screened off with furniture. The children work through a series of tasks on either computer, sometimes individually, sometimes in similar-aged pairs or with an older "mentor" teaching a younger child a new skill. The fax machine is used by the children to communicate regularly with other schools, including a small school in Scotland.

The teacher keeps a record of each child's use of the computer and logs their progress against a programme of activities designed to systematically develop IT skills. When possible, IT activities are integrated into class or group theme work, but on other occasions IT work is carried out for its own sake. At times, the teacher uses a "floor book" (a large A0-sized book which is placed on the floor in the middle of the group) to record children's contributions to discussions when working on collaborative IT activities.

A large inner-city infant school

Each teaching bay is equipped with two computers. All computers are interlinked through a network to a central hard drive (server) on which all the school's software is stored. The main content-free packages such as the word processor (Word) and spreadsheet (Excel) are configured in three ways for different age bands. The school presently has one stand-alone computer linked to the Internet but the IT co-ordinator intends to provide Internet access for all computers in the coming year.

The children use the computers as and when needed, mostly for word processing. The teachers track each child's computer use electronically. As the children log on to the network, their names, the date, amount of time spent on the computer, and pieces of software used is recorded in a file which the teacher can access.

In addition to the "everyday" IT use, each half-term's topic focus includes specific IT-related activities aimed at addressing particular strands to progressively develop IT skills and knowledge.

One thing all these examples have in common is that the teachers have thought carefully about the use of IT in their classrooms. In most cases, the school or infant department has a well-structured approach to the use of IT and systems in place for supporting teachers' planning and their assessment and recording of children's progress (see Chapter 7).

Managing the resources

Space

Informal studies have indicated that significantly more use is made of a computer when it has a permanent fixed site in a teaching area than when it is mobile. Points to consider when positioning a computer include the following.

- The location of power sockets, though, to some extent, the use of an extension lead can overcome some of the setbacks of inconsiderate classroom design
- Providing a clear field of view of the computer screen for the teacher to monitor children's progress and to be able to assist or intervene at opportune moments
- Making sure the screen and keyboard are at the correct height for children to use comfortably (and to comply with Health and Safety regulations)
- Avoiding reflected glare on the screen from a bright light source such as an outside window
- Obstructing the view of the screen by other children to minimise distraction
- Keeping resources near at hand (concept keyboard and overlays, printer, spare

printer paper, children's floppy disks, program disks (for non-hard-disk based machines), usage chart or log book)

People

The following questions might prove useful when pairing children for computer work.

- *Task* – Does the purpose of the activity affect the type of pairing? For example, will both children be collaborating on one outcome or assisting each other with their own separate pieces of work?
- *Child* – How might personalities or levels of IT capability affect the pairings? A less dominant or inexperienced child might be given insufficient opportunity to develop her skills and knowledge if her partner monopolises the keyboard.
- *Teacher* – Will some children need focused teaching to enable them to carry out the activity or make progress? Could a more experienced child assist one who is less experienced with a new aspect of learning – if so, is the more experienced child clear about her role?

Research by Culley (quoted in Boyd-Barrett and Scanlon, 1990) has shown that able children use the computer more often in primary classrooms than their less able classmates, as computer activities are often used as a reward or time-filler for those who have completed other work. However, it has been shown that children with learning difficulties gain far more from appropriately targeted IT work than more able children (e.g. see Hawkridge & Vincent, 1992). The teacher will need to ensure that all children are given appropriate access to the computer to suit individual needs.

The deployment of adults is another important consideration. It is not always convenient for the teacher to be regularly monitoring children at the computer, particularly when there are another 30 children demanding her attention. The use of well-briefed classroom assistants or parent helpers is an approach which many schools adopt.

The teacher of one Year 1 class has a regular rota of parent helpers who are timetabled to assist specifically with IT work. Each child has a record book in which both the parent helpers and the teacher write comments about the activities covered and the level of skill reached. Before each session the teacher also writes in the book the next activity and its purpose. The teacher holds regular sessions for the helpers in which IT skills and knowledge are shared and the teacher reinforces the educational objectives for planned activities.

Time

The most valuable resource available to the teacher is time. This is particularly true for IT activities.

In their early work with the keyboard, children take considerably longer to write even the shortest piece of text than it would for them to write it by hand. It could be said that no piece of word processing is ever really completed as it can be redrafted and edited with ease. Children need time to continue working on a piece of IT work, to hone and perfect it.

To make the most of children's computer time, teachers use some of the following strategies.

- Using the computer only for short, intensive pieces of individual or paired work – captions, letters, poems, paragraphs, posters, small illustrations, short compositions, focused LOGO procedures, etc.
- Having children contributing to collaborative tasks – e.g. each pair writing one paragraph or page of a story, different pairs working on different aspects of a multimedia presentation, separate contributions to a jointly produced newsletter
- Using parent helpers to type in all or some of the children's text, then supporting the children as they edit and redraft
- Providing partially completed text files or computerised word banks (see Chapter 4, – "English and IT".

- Encouraging children to work repeatedly on a piece of quality work over an extended period of time
- Setting up a fixed rota of children's computer use which provides ample time (up to an hour for older infants) to engage in activities of greater depth
- Allowing children to work for as long as necessary on an activity, either until completion or until interest or enthusiasm wanes

Material resources

In addition to the hardware, resources include software, notes, literature and support materials. In Chapter 3, we examined ways in which children might store the outcome of their IT work – either using hard-disk files or floppy disks. Clearly, the ease with which children save and retrieve their partially completed work is of vital importance if they are to use IT as a tool. Organising classroom IT resources and making sure the children are given clear instructions and encouragement in their use will do much to develop the children's IT capability and help them become independent of the teacher. As one teacher put it: "I don't have any problems with the computer. The children sort them out for me."

This sort of confidence does not happen by chance.

Medium-term planning and IT activities

Ideally, all medium-term planning ought to be based on the school's scheme of work (see Chapter 7). If one does not exist, a teacher would be wise to devise her own (year-long) long-term plan. Medium-term planning in IT is a lot easier if it is based on a carefully thought-out scheme of work, as IT straddles so many other areas of the curriculum.

What is medium-term planning?

In some schools, a medium-term plan covers a whole school year or a term while others prefer to plan half-termly topics. Medium-term planning is sometimes carried out collaboratively by clusters of teachers agreeing common objectives for IT activities within similar age bands. Other schools have such clearly laid out long-term schemes of work that collaborative planning is less necessary.

IT is a difficult curriculum area to monitor as it does not often have a discrete place on the timetable. For this reason, having a well-ordered approach to medium-term planning is beneficial, not only for the teacher, but for a school's IT co-ordinator in monitoring IT coverage across the school.

Topic: Jim and the Beanstalk **Class:** 7

Week	**English**	**Maths**	**Science**	**D& T**
Week 1 (wb 5/3/96)	Giant and tiny words - Giant poems	Measuring activities (Giant measurements)	Bean planting - finding out about plants	Introducing the Giant problem
IT	Word processing poems (Red and Blue Groups)	None	Using CD ROM (Class lesson)	None
Week 2 (wb 12/3/96)	Giant poems	Measuring (Tiny measurements)	Bean experiments	Planning the Giant display
IT	Word processing poems (Green & Yellow Groups)	None	None	Giant Adventure (Red & Blue Groups)
Week 3 (wb 19/3/96	Giant story	Measuring ourselves	Measuring bean plants - sorting beans	Making giant glasses and book

Figure 6.1 Part of a medium-term planning grid

Approaches to medium-term planning

Planning grid
One common approach which many schools adopt is to set out the objectives and activities for a specified time period in the form of a grid.

The column headings vary from school to school, but the purpose tends to remain the same however the grid is laid out: to help ensure a balance of coverage across the curriculum and to maintain coherence and continuity. This is particularly useful for IT work which, since 1995, has to be incorporated into all subject areas.

Theme plans
Another approach which is used for medium-term planning which is sometimes combined with the planning grid is the "theme plan" or "termly forecast". Each of the subject areas is addressed in turn, providing detailed information about aims and objectives, intended practice and resource requirements.

This highly detailed approach is very useful for subject areas with which a teacher is unfamiliar or lacking in confidence – which is sometimes the case with IT work. If the IT co-ordinator has access to this sort of detailed planning by teachers, she can make suggestions as to ways in which IT work can be extended or further enhanced in colleagues' classroom activities.

Planning sheet

Period covered: 16 April-27 May 1996

Theme: Jim and the Beanstalk

Subject: English **Class:** 7

Educational objectives
- develop poetry appreciation and writing
- develop story writing skills (planning, plot)
- develop vocabulary (size related words)
- introduce collaborative writing

Contribution to IT objectives
- improve word processing skills (editing text)

Development
Week 1 - Introduce story of Jim and the Beanstalk
Vocabulary work - Big and little words
Collaborative poetry writing on the word processor (Blue and Red Groups)

Week 2

Figure 6.2 An example of theme planning for English, showing the IT aspect

Short term planning

Short-term planning can be the scribbled notes a teacher makes for her own benefit prior to a lesson through to the more formalised lesson notes which student teachers are expected to prepare prior to their work in the classroom. For short-term planning of IT to be effective, the following points need to be considered.

- What is the educational purpose of the activity – to develop IT capability, to support learning in another area of the curriculum, or both?
- Will the children need to be monitored to identify opportune moments for teacher intervention to enhance their skills?
- Does it provide children with experience of using IT as a tool?
- Are there opportunities to assess children's IT competence?
- Will the children work co-operatively or collaboratively? How will this be introduced and supported?

Approaches to short-term planning

Figures 6.3 and 6.4 are examples of teachers' short-term planning notes for IT. To what extent do you feel they address each of the above questions?

IT Activity
Fish pictures for water topic

- familiarisation with Paintspa
- mouse practice

Working in pairs (older and younger child)
Draw a fish using only three colours

Make sure they can all:

control mouse	print picture
use palette to choose colours	save picture

Figure 6.3 An example of lesson planning in note form

Clowns topic - IT Activities

1. English

Activity: Word processing clown descriptions

Purposes

a. to develop word processing skills - cutting, moving and pasting
bold, italic and underline

b. to make more use of descriptive vocabulary (adjectives and adverbs)

c. to practise saving and printing

d. (for some children) merging pictures and text

Development

1. Brainstorming - whole class session, using poems, pictures and own ideas to make a vocabulary list of clown words. these words will be typed on to a word processor file by me at the end of the day - words put into groups (colours, mood words, describing words (adjectives), action words (verbs and adverbs).
2. Explain activity to all - demonstrate cutting and pasting - reminder about bold and italic
3. Children working in pairs on the computer. Using word lists as basis for own writing (Mrs Smith to assist when available - arrange group so least confident use computer when she's there)
4. Children who have drawn clown pictures merge their pictures with text (Teacher to work with each group as required)
5. Print out and save work at the end of each session (Experienced children to assist less experienced)

Assessment opportunities

1. Liaise with Mrs Smith - monitor skills with cutting, pasting and using text styles (esp. Lions group) (a)
2. Assess confidence with which new skill (file merging) is learned and used (d)
3. Check all can save and print without help (c)
   Check work for imaginative use of adjectives and adverbs (b)

Resources

1. Whiteboard and marker, poetry books (Project collection), clown pictures, video?
2. Computer with word processor (Full Phase)
3. Ditto
4. Ditto plus desks with clown pictures
5. Ditto plus printer and children's work disks

Figure 6.4 An example of one teacher's detailed planning notes

Neither example is presented as an ideal model of short-term planning as they were intended to be for the teacher's own use and not for "public" consumption. Each of the teachers is, however, a highly successful classroom practitioner and makes good use of IT.

The most effective teaching is not only well planned, it makes the most of opportunities that arise to move children on at important moments.

Monitoring and teacher intervention

The timely intervention of the teacher can not only have a beneficial effect on the development of children's technical skills and knowledge of IT, it can be used to help develop children's higher order thinking skills. In a study by Hill and Browne (1988), the quality of the talk of groups of 6- and 7-year-old children working round a computer on an adventure program (*Granny's Garden* (4mation)) was shown to be enhanced by the intervention of the teacher. The best form of intervention appeared to be that which focused children's attention on significant information and used carefully structured questioning to promote reasoning, logical thinking and prediction.

Teachers often feel torn between showing children what to do and letting them find out for themselves. Vygotsky's (1962) work suggests children make more and better progress if they are sensitively supported by an adult. A teacher's interventions will be more effective if they not only take account of where the child is now, but also where she ought to be going next.

How, when and why should a teacher intervene?

The type and level of intervention is dependent upon a number of factors:

- *The purpose and nature of the task in hand*
  All IT activities require some intervention by the teacher, either to check on progress or to introduce new skills and knowledge at the most opportune moments. Having a clearly defined purpose for the task will help sharpen the focus of the teacher's interventions.
- *The extent of the children's familiarity with the software and hardware*
  Better for the children to work with a small number of versatile programs and progressively develop skills and confidence in these through carefully structured activities than trying to learn how to use large numbers of programs superficially.
- *The personalities and aptitudes of the children*
  This will affect the grouping of the children and the level of challenge set by the task.
- *The teacher's knowledge of and confidence with IT*
  Being familiar with a program will help the teacher identify the circumstances when children are ready to move on to a new feature or to use the software for a more demanding purpose.

Of these points, the most important is the last. You might find the following points reassuring.

- It is more important for a teacher to know how to use a computer for educational purposes than how computers work.
- Using a small number of content-free programs well (e.g. word processor, desktop publishing package, spreadsheet) is more successful than trying to use a wide range of software.
- The more powerful modern computers and software are easier to use than the computers which were originally supplied to schools.
- Making mistakes when using a computer is part of the learning process. Experienced users have simply devised more strategies for coping with and avoiding mistakes – but they still make them.
- It is difficult to damage a computer, unless physical violence is used (but try to avoid the temptation).

- Teachers who use IT themselves are more confident and successful in their teaching than those who do not.
- In-service education is crucial to the successful use of IT in the classroom (see Hall & Rhodes, 1988; IMPACT, 1994). Approaches to INSET are discussed in Chapter 7.

Monitoring and assessment

The monitoring and assessment of IT work requires a slightly different approach to that required for other classroom activities owing to the unique nature of the relationship between the learner and the computer. Some programs, most notably the drill-and-practice type (see Chapter 3), include systems for recording children's responses. While these provide some means of assessing progress with non-IT skills, they cannot measure the development of children's IT capability. The way in which children's IT work is monitored and assessed is dependent upon the purpose of the assessment. Will the results be used formatively, to help guide immediate or subsequent teaching; diagnostically, to help identify or anticipate problems; or summatively, to measure the child's present level of performance – or a combination of the three?

OFSTED (1995) inspections have found that there is a tendency for primary schools to record children's *experience* with IT rather than assessing *achievement*. It is easier to observe and record what children have done, but less easy to assess what has been learned. To assess IT capability, a teacher has to consider each child's:

- level of skill in using the hardware – keyboard(s), mouse, disk drives, printer;
- competency in using a range of software and applications;
- ability to overcome technical difficulties when using the computer;
- ability to apply general understanding of the way computer programs work to new pieces of software;
- confidence in making decisions about whether the computer could assist them with a task, and knowledge of which pieces of software might be appropriate;
- understanding of the way computers contribute to problem solving in the world at large.

The first three items are relatively easy to assess, but the final three throw up problems which are particular to assessment in IT. How can these problems be overcome?

Strategies for assessing children's IT capability

- Make use of well-briefed parent helpers to work exclusively with children at the computer, recording the amount of help each child received with a piece of work.
- Devise methods of enabling the children to monitor and record their own progress, e.g. self-assessment sheets of skills accomplished in illustrated or written form – e.g. "I can print a page."
- Question children and ask them to demonstrate how they went about a task.
- Set occasional prescribed challenges – e.g. "Can you write a caption and print it out for me?"
- Vary pairings to see how children work with other partners.
- Encourage children to save their first drafts as well as final drafts of each piece of IT work.
- Provide opportunities to solve problems with IT at regular intervals and give different children different roles.
- Role play can provide models of the use of IT use in the wider world and encourage discussion.

The most effective way for a teacher to assess a child's IT capability is to informally observe the children working on purposeful activities in meaningful contexts. A teacher's enthusiasm for, interest in and confidence with IT will have a profound effect on the attitudes and responses of the children.

Recording progress

A teacher's record-keeping system needs to reflect two perspectives – the areas of the curriculum that her teaching has covered and the progress of individual children. Although related, the two facets are distinct – what has been taught is not always the same as what has been learned.

Recording teaching

The level of detail which is used is largely dependent upon the purpose to which the record will be put:

- to act as an *aide-mémoire* for the teacher,
- to assist the teacher with future planning,
- to communicate curriculum coverage to colleagues,
- to inform replacement teachers.

Most teachers use their medium- and short-term planning as the basis for their teaching records. An outline of discrepancies between what was planned and what was actually taught makes efficient use of teachers' time. Some schools back this up with checklists or charts indicating which sections of the school's scheme of work have been covered.

The advantage of a charting system such as this is that it is relatively easy to analyse which areas of the curriculum have been covered and where there are any gaps or overemphases. The disadvantage is that it lacks detail as to how the aspect or strand has been taught or the level of depth of the children's learning. Such a record is useful for gaining an overview but is no substitute for a system which shows the extent of children's learning.

Recording children's progress

For a recording system to be effective it has to balance detail with ease and economy of use.

Computer-based records

Schools which have computerised their record systems (e.g. *PIMS* (*Primary Information Management System*) (Longman Logotron)) find there are advantages in having immediate and flexible access to information about individuals or groups of children. However, setting up such a system does require enthusiasm, hard work, commitment and some outlay of time and financial resources.

	EY			Y1			Y2		
IT skills	Controlling mouse	Locating keys	Using space bar / shift Printing out	Loading own programs		Saving own files and loading them		Merging picture files with text	
Word processing	Using CK for phrases		Writing captions and labels	Writing short poems (using word bank)		Varying size and style of text	Cutting and pasting text	Multimedia (story)	Simple formatting (tab / indent)
Graphics	Scribble pictures	My World topic pictures		Shape patterns	Represent-ational paintings		Editing / zoom	Multimedia (story)	
Sound / Music		Listening unit		Recording sounds (tape recorder)			Compose World (for play)	Multimedia (story)	Interviewing people (tape recorder)
Database work	Non-computer investigation	CD ROM intro. (Teddy)		Ourselves database	CD ROM (information seeking)	Foods survey			Investigation (Local study)
Modelling			My World simulation (dressing)			Adventure (Playground)		Multimedia (story)	
Control			Roamer (Toytown)		Roamer (Mazes)	Tiny LOGO intro.	LOGO pictures	LOGO challenges	LOGO problems

Figure 6.5 A school's IT curriculum coverage chart based on its scheme of work

Individual portfolios

These often include annotated examples of children's work and detailed information about the child's progress in all curriculum areas. Print-outs of children's IT work will often not communicate the quality of work which went into it, unless the teacher adds explanatory comments. The more detailed a child's portfolio becomes, the less likely it will be used as a source of information to help inform subsequent teaching.

Individual checklists of progress

Similar to the curriculum coverage chart, some schools use checklists to record each child's progress. These are sometimes included in the children's portfolios to provide an overview of progress. Not only are these time-consuming to complete for a whole class, they tend to record experience rather than achievement. Furthermore, the effort required to use individual lists as a basis for planning future activities in IT is daunting.

Group records

One teacher uses her medium-term group planning sheet as the basis for her group record (see Figure 6.6). She runs four groups of about eight children and has three children with individual educational plans who sometimes integrate with one of the groups. At the end of the half-term, she assesses the children's responses to the activities and completes a record for each group as a whole. Eight copies of each group record are made and one is placed in each child's progress folder. She adds individual notes when a child has responded differently to others in the group. The groupings and activities for the next topic are adjusted according to the teacher's assessment of the children's progress.

Although there are some drawbacks, a group recording system does appear to offer a compromise between detail and manageability. It balances the detailed yet time-consuming approach of recording individual attainment with the more manageable but less informative whole class curriculum-coverage records.

Reporting

A group of 20 primary teachers on an INSET course for IT felt the following to be the most important information about a child's progress and performance in IT:

- What a child can do
- What experience a child has had in IT
- What special accomplishments the child has achieved
- Any difficulties the child has experienced
- What the child will need to do next

A group of 22 parents of primary-aged children felt they wanted to know:

- what level their child has reached,
- how their child is performing in relation to others, and
- what they can do to help their child improve.

Although there are dangers in generalising from small samples, there would appear at first glance to be some discrepancy between what the parents require and what the teachers feel they ought to know. A closer examination reveals that the information required by the two groups is principally the same, only the emphasis differs.

What the child can do, what experience she has had and her special accomplishments provide a clear indication for the teacher of the child's level of achievement. However, whereas the teacher has access to national and school-based measures of performance, most parents do not. Some means of communicating where a child is, in relation to the planned school or national curriculum, is what most parents would like to see.

IT skills	Loading own programs	Saving own files and loading them	Other
Comments			
Word processing	Short poems (using word bank)	Varying size and style of text	Other
Comments			
Graphics	Shape patterns	Paintings	Other
Comments			
Sound/Music	Recording sounds	Other	
Comments			
Database work	Ourselves database	CD ROM (info seeking)	Food Survey
Comments			
Modelling	Use of Adventure	Other	
Comments			
Control	Roamer (Mazes)	Tiny LOGO skills	Other
Comments			

Figure 6.6 An example of a group record for IT

Compare these two reports on the same child.

Jackie has made good progress with IT this year. She uses the keyboard with confidence, can save and load her own work and is able to use the printer without assistance. She has written poems with a word processor and has drawn some very attractive pictures using a graphics package using the mouse. She has had some experience of using a database to draw graphs but will need to develop this further next year. Jackie has worked hard this year and enjoys her work on the computer.

Jackie is making steady progress with IT. As we would expect for a child of her age, she uses the keyboard with confidence, can save and load her own work and is able to use the printer without assistance. Whereas her word-processing skills are developing appropriately and she is well in advance with graphics work (her computer-drawn pictures show considerable skill and dexterity), she has not made as much progress as we would have liked with handling data. Although she has had some experience of using a database to draw graphs she will need to develop this further next year. Jackie enjoys her work on the computer. She is more confident with creative work on the computer but needs to work just as hard with using the computer in maths and science work.

The first extract is more descriptive whereas the second is more evaluative. Whereas the first is quite meaningful for the teacher who has access to the school's schemes of work, the second gives parents some indication as to whether the progress Jackie is making is appropriate. At the parents' interview, more detail can be expressed regarding what is thought of as "appropriate" or "expected". These statements can only be made where a school and its teachers have a clear and agreed understanding of what the children should have learned and ought to be learning next.

The teacher as a user of IT

In 1996 and 1997 the Department for Education and Employment funded a scheme to provide teachers with their own laptop computers (the Portables for Teachers Project). It has been recognised that, for teachers to be confident and skilful in developing children's skills and knowledge of IT, teachers need first-hand experience of the positive contribution computers can make to their work.

In what ways could an infant teacher make use of a computer for her own work?

Word-processing documentation

The most widespread use of the personal computer is for word processing or desktop publishing. Many schools now word process all their policy documents because they realise that their documentation will be likely to be amended regularly. But policy documentation is not the only area of a teacher's work which is paper based.

Producing high-quality worksheets

Once a worksheet has been produced with a word processor, graphics or desktop publishing package, it can be readily modified:

- to improve its effectiveness in the light of experience;
- to individualise activities for various ability groups;
- to act as a template for similar worksheets serving different purposes;
- for distribution to other classes, to form the basis for school-based INSET, or to circulate ideas to neighbouring schools at support group meetings;
- to form the basis for a school resource to augment or replace commercial publications.

Other uses

In addition to producing good quality worksheets, teachers make use of their computers for some or all of the following.

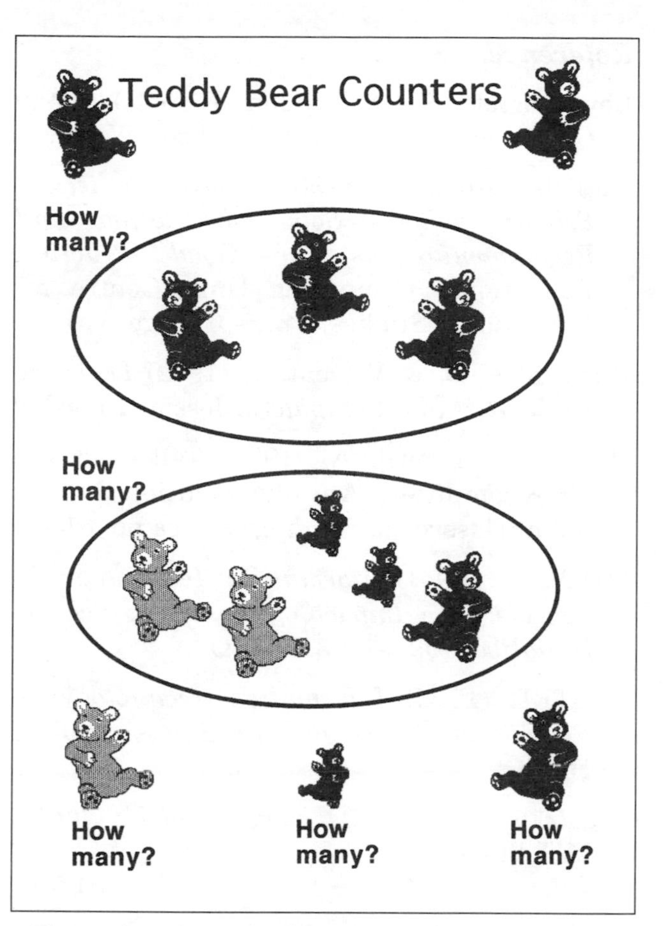

Figure 6.7 A teacher's worksheet produced with graphics and clip-art

- *As an information source* – CD ROM based encyclopaedias and data bases provide a wealth of information and ideas for activities for children and can assist a teacher with planning the content of her work.
- *To gain access to the Internet* – There are a number of support networks through which teachers and children can share ideas or seek information.
- *Record keeping* – There are systems which exist for primary schools which assist in the process of recording pupils' progress at the classroom or whole-school level. Some generate generalised annual reports which can be embellished by the teacher (e.g. *PIMS* (Longman Logotron), *Report Writer* (CCS), *Class Lists* (Soft Teach)).
- *Grading books for readability* – For teachers and schools who grade children's literature for readability, a useful piece of software such as *Readability Reckoning* (Arnold Wheaton/AVP) or *Text Grader 2* (Stanley Thornes) is worth considering.
- *Diagnosis of children's learning difficulties* – Software exists which can be used to help diagnose particular learning difficulties and suggest possible remediation strategies (see Chapter 3, "IT and Special Educational Needs").
- *Preparing, trouble shooting, assessing or developing children's IT work* – With a home computer compatible with that in the classroom, teachers can prepare and assess IT work away from the pressures of the classroom.

The teacher's computer

Since the introduction of pocket or palmtop computers (e.g. Psion Series 3 or Acorn Pocket Book) and the increased availability of laptop computers, it is easier than ever for computers to be transported between home and school. Alternatively, if a teacher can afford her own home computer, which is compatible with that used in school, all she needs to take home is a floppy disk containing the saved files of the children's work.

Not only does ownership and use of a computer increase the teacher's knowledge and confidence; a teacher who regularly uses a computer is a valuable role model for children.

Summary

Managing IT use in the classroom is not without its problems – mostly associated with resourcing and assessment. However, in developing their IT capability, children should increasingly become more independent of the teacher. It is interesting to note that, although children will seldom offer or accept assistance from each other with other classroom activities, they are far more willing to co-operate and be mutually supportive when making use of the computer.

Teacher intervention is very important for IT activities. Children make more rapid progress and become independent more quickly when teachers provide assistance at critical moments. A teacher should therefore continually monitor children's IT work in the same way as she would oversee all the activities ongoing in her classroom.

Assessment, planning, record keeping and reporting are so closely related that, to keep the systems manageable, they should be addressed together to help ensure that each aspect supports the other. Although assessment is more complicated with IT, it is achievable, provided activities are planned and monitored to include opportunities for monitoring, assessment. Assessment should be closely linked to forward planning

In the next chapter we examine wider school-based issues associated with policy, planning and practice.

References

Boyd-Barrett, O. & Scanlon, E. (eds) (1990) *Computers and Learning*; Addison Wesley

Hall, J. & Rhodes, V. (1988) *Microcomputers in Primary Schools: Some Observations and Recommendations for Good Practice*; Educational Computing Unit, Centre for Educational Studies, King's College

Hawkridge, D. & Vincent, T. (1992) *Learning Difficulties and Computers*; Jessica Kingsley

Hill, A. & Brown, A. (1988) Talk and the Microcomputer: An investigation in the infant classroom; *Reading*, 22 (1); pp. 61 – 9

IMPACT (1994) *Information Technology in Schools: The Impact of the IT in Schools Initiative*, 1990–1993; HMSO

OFSTED (1995) *Information Technology: A Review of Inspection Findings*, 1993/4; HMSO

Vygotsky, L. S. (1962) *Thought and Language*; MIT Press

7 The school and IT

What this chapter is about

This chapter concentrates on the implications of IT for the whole school. It provides information about:

- the review and development of school policy;
- equal opportunities and IT;
- the scheme of work for IT;
- INSET and IT – including ideas for effective school-based INSET;
- the OFSTED inspection process and IT;
- home-school links and IT.

School policy

The process by which a policy statement comes into being is in many ways more valuable than the document itself, provided the policy is drawn up in discussion with the whole staff. Recognising the school's strengths and weaknesses and negotiating agreement on a set of aims and objectives can help generate a common understanding of what IT education is all about.

The unique character of IT education sets the IT policy apart from other areas of the curriculum. The policy statement should at least reflect and address this, particularly showing how:

- IT capability must be taught through all subjects of the curriculum (except PE);
- children should be given opportunities to use IT as a tool to solve problems and learn about aspects of the curriculum;
- the interactive nature of the computer and its software affects the way children learn.

The content of a policy statement for IT

The principal purpose of a policy statement is to set out what the school believes to be important and indicate its intentions. It should be visionary, yet realistic and achievable. The following suggested headings might assist in drawing up, evaluating or reviewing a policy statement. Bear in mind the wider definition of IT which encompasses more than the use of computers.

Introduction

Setting out the structure of the document and indicating something about the special nature of IT education (see Chapters 1 and 2).

Aims

Laying down what the school intends to achieve through IT education. Aims might cover such aspects as:

- Developing skills, knowledge and understanding to enable the confident, independent application of IT to tasks
- Progressively and systematically developing technical skills in the use of hardware and software
- Extending skills in communicating and handling information with, through and without IT
- Developing confidence and strategies for problem solving
- Fostering enjoyment and satisfaction
- Developing positive attitudes and confidence
- Nurturing social skills through collaborative group work
- Providing a medium for creative and imaginative activity
- Appreciating the purpose, value and problems of using IT in everyday life

The school's approach to IT

An overview of the ways in which the aims are put into practice. This might include:

- Teaching approaches and classroom organisation
- The provision, availability and organisation of resources, including some indication of future plans and priorities
- The content and organisation of the IT curriculum
- The integration of IT across the curriculum
- The procedures for the assessment, recording and reporting of IT capability
- The provision and use of IT for children with special educational needs
- Strategies for ensuring equality of opportunity for all children and the promotion of non-stereotypical images of IT use (see below)

Success criteria

The evidence, outcomes and indicators by which the school will judge its effectiveness in the promotion of its aims.

Appendices

Some schools append the IT co-ordinator's job description and a full list of current and planned resource and INSET provision.

Owing to the pace of change in IT and IT education, a policy statement will need regular review – at least once every three years. A review might focus on the following.

- The extent to which the school is meeting its aims for IT
- An audit of actual IT use in classrooms
- The effectiveness of teaching strategies and approaches
- The appropriateness of existing resources
- INSET needs in the light of the above

The outcome of the review might be a shift of emphasis in school policy or the hardening of a school's resolve to develop more effective approaches to achieving its agreed objectives. The review should feed into the school's development plan, setting targets through a dated action plan.

Equal opportunities

At some point, the management team of a school will need to audit and monitor computer use to ensure equal opportunities are provided for all pupils.

- Do children who are registered as having special educational needs have sufficient software for their use?
- Is there a need for software or hardware for children with physical or sensory impairment?
- Is there a need for software in other languages besides English?
- In a random sweep of the school at any one moment, are more of one group (e.g. boys, more able children) using computers than others?
- Are teaching strategies ensuring equality of access for all groups of pupils?
- What role models are presented to the children in computer use and trouble-shooting – in person and through software, support material and literature?
- To what extent is IT used across the curriculum in each age group? Is there a tendency for some subjects to be over represented? How might this affect access for some children?

The school's policy should indicate the strategies in place for addressing these aspects and any others which might be specific to the school's individual circumstances (e.g. a large proportion of children from one ethnic group, any particular children with specific learning difficulties).

Long-term planning – the scheme of work

The scheme of work describes how the IT policy will be put into practice in the school. It should:

- show how IT capability will be progressively and continuously developed through the school;
- indicate the actual hardware, software and activities which will be used;
- be used by all teachers to guide or determine their medium- and short-term planning;
- be drawn up by all teachers in collaboration or at least through consultation;
- be down to earth, realistic, practicable and useful;
- reviewed and updated regularly (at least every year – or two years where schools have rolling programmes of themes).

The ideal scheme of work is one which best meets the needs of the staff within a school. It should be a working document which teachers feel able to refer to, make use of and contribute to on an ongoing basis. The best schemes of work are those to which all staff have contributed and which they feel reflect their actual and intended classroom practices.

Examples of schemes of work

Figures 7.1 and 7.2 are based on schemes of work seen in a number of infant and primary schools. They represent the two main forms of schemes – the "grid" and the "catalogue". Some schools combine the two forms by summarising the school's scheme in a grid and providing more detail in a catalogue.

Those who favour the grid-based approach argue that it is concise, easy to refer to and emphasises progression. It is also seen to be helpful when making assessments and when linking planning with assessment. Its major disadvantage is that it lacks detail, particularly for teachers with insufficient confidence or experience with IT.

The term "catalogue" sums up the advantages of this approach to describing the school's scheme of work – it has the potential to become very comprehensive and highly detailed. The disadvantage is that the overall plan or structure of the scheme can become lost in the detail. This is why a combination of both approaches is often adopted by schools: a grid for ease of reference and guidance with a catalogue for reassurance and detail.

In drawing up the content of a scheme of work, some co-ordinators find it easier to start with what they expect the oldest children to achieve and working backwards. For those who are devising or reviewing a scheme of work, Chapter 2 provides suggestions for progression in each of the strands while Chapters 4 and 5 provide details of activities which can be organised to achieve those objectives. The following questions may help guide the evaluation of a scheme of work.

- How prescriptive should it be? Do teachers need a clear set of stages through which to progress and detailed information about activities, or just general guidance on making effective use of their existing expertise? Should it be a recipe to be followed, a skeleton to be fleshed out by the teachers or a comprehensive quarry of ideas?
- Have all the strands been covered and sufficiently well developed? Is the National Curriculum being addressed? If gaps exist, does this reflect insufficient resources, lack of expertise or an already overcrowded curriculum? How should the gaps be filled?
- How fully has IT been integrated into the curriculum? Could IT be used to support, enhance or extend existing work in other subjects? (See Chapters 4 and 5.)
- What are the areas of strength in the school curriculum? Are there opportunities here for building on good practice through the integration of IT? Could areas of weakness in the school be enhanced by use of IT?
- Is the scheme of work achievable? Does the school have sufficient resources, time,

Nonesuch County Infant School

IT Scheme of Work – Year 1 Rolling Programme Cycle

	IT skills	Word processing	Graphics	Sound/Music	Database work	Modelling	Control
Nursery	Introduction to the computer Mouse control		Scribble pictures		CD ROM Noisy House		
Early years Myself	Locating keys Mouse for moving objects and cursor	Using CK for phrases Inserting words				My World simulation (dressing)	
Nursery Rhymes	Loading programs			Listening unit (Nursery rhymes and folk tales)	Retrieving images, sound and text CD ROM (Talking books)		Tape recorder controls
Homes					Non-computer investigation (Our Homes)		
Toys	Fine mouse control Typing words and phrases Use of shift and space bar	Captions for toy pictures	Drawing with shapes Shape patterns				
Growth	Intro. to spreadsheet Interpreting data Manipulating graphs				Recording bean growth on spreadsheet		
Journeys	Sequencing commands						Roamer (Pathways)

Y1 School and Grounds	Saving own files and loading them		Representational paintings Use of tools (Paintbrush)	Recording sounds (tape recorder)			
Humans and Animals	Inserting and moving text Keyboard skills (increased speed) Printing out	Short poems (using word bank)			Storing information (All about Me) Retrieving information (CD ROMs) Animals		Video recorder controls
Moving things	Sequencing instructions						Roamer (Moving)
Our History							Simple circuits (Science topic)
Growth	Increased mouse control		Editing/zoom (Growing pics)				
Our Community	Paragraphs of writing	Descriptive writing					Roamer (Maps)
Y2 Our Neighbours	Editing skills	Cutting and pasting text (prepared files)					Tiny LOGO intro. LOGO pictures
Humans and Other Animals					Ourselves database CD ROM (information seeking)		
Forces and Motion						Adventure (Playground)	LOGO challenges
Life in the Past		Varying size and style of text		Compose World (for play)		My World topic pictures	
Plants		Simple formatting (tab/indent)			Food survey		LOGO problems
People, Jobs and Leisure	Merging picture files with text		Clip art Multimedia	Interviewing people (tape recorder) Multimedia	Investigation (Local study)	My World topic pictures Multimedia	

Figure 7.1 grid-based scheme of work

Avon Infant School *IT Scheme of Work – Page 3*

Ourselves

Communicating Information strand
Word processing

Stage 1 – Keyboard familiarisation

Captions for portraits using concept keyboard or typed in

Titles for topic sections

Sequencing phrases for everyday activities (getting dressed, cleaning teeth, coming to school), using CK overlays (see resource file)

Stage 2 – Using space bar and shift – mouse (arrow keys) to position cursor

Diary sequences as captions

Paragraphs using word banks (Full Phase – see library disk for samples)

Stage 3 – Increasing speed and accuracy of typing – simple editing

Class questionnaire (typed in by teacher, modified by children)

Letters to Father Christmas (provide letter format, children enter own text)

Software

Stylus (BBC B)
There are some ready-made overlays in the resources room (Parts of the body, Clothes, Getting dressed, My house) with files that can be used straight away. There is an instruction sheet to remind you how to make your own CK overlays with Stylus (it's very easy).

Full Phase (Acorn)
There are no ready-made word banks for Ourselves – teachers make their own based in brainstorming with the children or using spelling lists.

Desktop Publishing

This enables children to combine text and pictures on the same page.

Stage 1 – Entering text and manipulating images separately

See word processing and image processing

Stage 2 – Using a dedicated story writing package (Desktop Stories)

The Desktop Stories picture file includes a boy and a girl who can represent the children. A story about Our Adventure could form part of the topic.

Stage 3 – Improving text and image processing

See word processing and image processing

Stage 4 – Importing pictures into a word processor

Using photos of children from Photo CD and making wanted posters

Using photos and writing short autobiographies

Figure 7.2 An extract from a "catalogue-based" scheme of work

expertise or commitment to carry it through into practice? Does the complete scheme of work need to be phased in over time and linked to school and staff development?

- What is the relationship between the scheme and assessment and recording? Can the recording process be linked with the scheme (e.g. can the same grid be used for planning and for recording individuals', ability groups', classes' or year-groups' progress? Can the scheme help link assessment with planning? (See Chapter 6.)
- How will the scheme be monitored and reviewed? What are the channels by which teachers can feed back information about its implementation? To what extent will the co-ordinator oversee the application and effectiveness of the scheme of work? When will the scheme next be reviewed, and by whom?

A scheme of work can never said to be complete, which is why it ought to be word processed. The most effective scheme of work is one which is used continually by teachers for reference and guidance. One which seldom sees the light of day is clearly not serving a useful purpose and should be abandoned or completely revised.

INSET

The first stage in any INSET process is the identification of staff needs – the areas which are in need of development or where gaps exist in expertise or provision. With devolved INSET budgets, schools can decide whether to have these needs addressed in-house or through external support.

School-based INSET

Few primary and infant schools are fortunate enough to have a large proportion of staff who are well-trained, confident users of IT. In the majority of schools, the expertise for IT lies in the hands of one or occasionally two teachers (see IMPACT, 1994; OFSTED, 1995). Schools which make effective use of existing expertise in IT usually have headteachers who are keen on IT and well-organised systems for sharing good practice in all areas of the curriculum. In some schools it was found that INSET money is spent on hardware rather than on staff training. Schools which are well resourced with IT equipment are not necessarily those which are using it most effectively.

Approaches to disseminating good IT practice in schools include the following:

- Displaying and discussing examples of children's IT work at staff meetings
- Holding "surgeries" in which teachers bring specific problems associated with IT to be discussed
- Having "celebrations" of good practice – then evaluating and analysing why these are successful and attempting to apply these principles to other areas
- Using professional development days to provide time and space for teachers to work extensively on computers (in pairs)
- Creating non-contact time for the IT co-ordinator to work alongside colleagues or team teach an aspect of IT
- Using non-contact time for teachers to work alongside the IT co-ordinator in her classroom
- Organising team teaching in which the IT co-ordinator works with another teacher and both sets of children on joint projects
- Video-taping exemplar lessons (video extracts should never exceed 15 minutes to maintain interest)
- Preparing support materials for each other to use, particularly if different teachers or year groups focus on different aspects of the school or IT curriculum

The "horizon effect" and how to overcome it

One difficulty of drawing only upon the expertise which exists within a school is what is known as the "horizon effect" (Hargreaves, 1989), which occurs when groups of teachers only see to the limits of their own experience and are unaware of what they don't yet know.

All schools need some input from outside their walls to broaden teachers' horizons. This can be achieved in several ways:

- Visiting or working with other schools – to find out others' solutions to your problems
- Reading publications – e.g. *Microscope,* the journal of Micros and Primary Education (MAPE); subscription currently £20.00 per year
- Using the Internet for finding teaching resources – e.g. Research Machines' Internet for Learning (IFL) site has a range of resources available for teachers
- Using the Internet to join newsgroups or for e-mail – many teachers now share their experiences on the Internet, ideas can be aired and someone will be bound to have a solution (or sympathy) for a problem
- Watching TV and video programmes – e.g. BBC's *Teaching for Today* and Channel 4's *Teaching for Tomorrow*
- Using distance learning packages – e.g. those produced by the Open University and the National Centre for Educational Technology (NCET);
- Attending conferences (e.g. MAPE Annual Conference) and sharing ideas
- Making use of outside support – e.g. buying in expertise from professional development centres, IT centres or local HE institutions

Centre-based INSET

The other way of overcoming the horizon effect is for teachers to attend meetings or courses. Centre-based courses tend to fall into one of four categories:

- Centrally funded courses or training programmes – e.g. Government (GEST)-funded courses for IT co-ordinators or to increase class teachers' expertise – usually run by LEAs
- LEA courses or sessions – these are now mostly funded through schools' INSET budgets
- Award-bearing courses (e.g. M.Ed.) – either funded through the school's INSET budget or by the individual teacher
- Interest group or cluster group meetings – voluntary self-help groups formed by enthusiastic teachers willing to share their experiences locally

The inspection process

If a school is being effective, it should be ready for an inspection at any moment in time. Its documentation, its procedures and the classroom practice of its teachers, though not perfect, will be at the optimum. For such a school, the greatest virtue of the inspection process lies in the objective overview which it provides. This should help the school identify which aspects are its strengths and which areas need to be developed. The two weakest areas of the curriculum in primary schools identified by inspectors have consistently been Design and Technology and Information Technology. Often, a school's glowing inspection report is marred by significant weaknesses in one or both of these aspects.

Preparing for inspection

Although little should be specially prepared for an inspection, it pays to make sure the school is ready. In the lead-up to an inspection, the teacher responsible for IT would probably want to attend to the following.

~ Is the documentation relating to IT up to date, presentable and available?

  Inspectors will expect to see:
  - The School Policy Document for IT
  - The Scheme of Work for IT
  - The IT co-ordinator's job description (if available)

~ Is the documentation coherent and consistent? Does what is said in the IT policy document tally with what is said in the others – particularly other subject policies and schemes of work?

~ Does the documentation reflect actual practice? If there are discrepancies, the IT co-ordinator may wish to add an explanatory appendix or clarify the situation in her co-ordinator's statement (see below).

- Has the IT co-ordinator prepared a written statement outlining how she puts her role into effect and cataloguing past achievements and future plans? Although not a requirement, it does help the inspector gain a picture of how IT is co-ordinated and organised through the school and could focus the inspection on issues which the co-ordinator would like to bring to the attention of the inspectors.
- Is all the equipment functioning properly? If there is a minor fault on a machine it might be wise to have it repaired well before the inspection.
- Have the teachers planned to include IT? How typical are their plans of usual IT usage? It may just be that the topics planned for the inspection period make only limited use of IT whereas normally there is a lot going on. The co-ordinator may wish to explain this in her statement.
- Has the co-ordinator prepared an up-to-date list of IT resources and the in-service training which she and the staff have received? It is very useful for the co-ordinator to have this sort of information to hand.
- Have the teachers kept examples of children's past IT work for inspectors to see? This is particularly important if, as above, the IT work during the inspection is untypical of what is normally being done.

It is rare for all a school's documentation to be complete and internally consistent. Curriculum policy statements and schemes of work are working documents and will inevitably be under review. Inspectors' primary concern is that teaching in classrooms is effective, consistent and progressively developing children's IT capability. Inspectors will be looking for evidence that what the school says it intends to do is carried through into practice. Five kinds of evidence are gathered:

1 *Documentation* – Virtually everything from the minutes of staff meetings to the amount of spending over the past few years on IT will be scrutinised.

2 *Observation* – Of teachers teaching and of children using the computers.

3 *Scrutiny of work* – Not only current work but examples from the previous term, or previous year if the inspection takes in the Autumn term.

4 *Discussions and interviews* – With individual teachers, classroom helpers, children and the IT co-ordinator (see below).

5 *Any other relevant information provided by the school.*

The co-ordinator's interview

The purpose of the interview is not to test or examine the co-ordinator's subject knowledge or IT expertise, its principal objective is to gather evidence and provide a communication channel for the co-ordinator. The co-ordinator ought to have an agenda prepared with a list of pointers which she feels should be mentioned. She might have already prepared a written statement providing an overview of her role and drawing attention to any significant events or accomplishments in the past year or two. This might help focus the inspector's attention on issues which the co-ordinator feels confident.

After the inspection

Once the inspection has finished, the staff will receive detailed informal feedback from the inspection team before the report is published. The report contains a condensed overview of the inspection findings for educational provision of the school covering all areas of the curriculum. A small number of key issues will be raised which the school will be required to address through an action plan drawn up by the governing body and the headteacher.

Home–school links

Parents sometimes hold some interesting misconceptions about the purpose of IT education in school. There are those who believe their children will learn how to program the computer and others who assume the children are allowed to play games all day. Most assume the computer acts as some form of substitute teacher.

Keeping parents informed

Schools have a number of communication channels through which information is passed to parents:

- Word of mouth, via the child
- Examples of work which the child takes home
- Informal conversations with the teacher before and after school
- Formal interviews/meetings with teachers
- Newsletters and notes
- Annual reports to parents about a child's progress
- The governing body's annual report and meeting
- The school's prospectus and/or brochure
- School policy documentation
- Children's records
- Parents' open evening(s)
- PTA and other social events (including school sports, concerts and plays)
- Curriculum meetings and workshops for parents

Consider how many of these could be used to demonstrate, illustrate or explain the children's use of IT. Practically all of them! The more opportunities parents have to see children and teachers using IT for everyday tasks, the more likely they will come to appreciate what the school is trying to achieve.

Home computing

It has been shown (e.g. by Martin, 1991) that children who use computers at home make significantly more progress with IT work than those who do not. The more parents are aware of how the school uses IT, the more likely home computing will contribute to the development of children's IT capability. A parents' IT workshop and/or information booklet could help develop the home–school partnership in the following ways.

- Informing parents about the role of IT in education (see Chapter 1 and policy document above)
- Providing examples of educational activities which can be carried out with generalised software such as word processors or graphics packages
- Suggesting pre-school computer-based activities with examples of software
- Demonstrating or explaining some of the other educational applications of IT (e.g. modelling with an adventure program, accessing information through CD ROM or the Internet, programming a turtle)
- Offering advice on the types of hardware and software which would be suitable for home use
- Advising parents on how to intervene to enhance the educational value of an IT activity
- Giving an indication of progression in IT skills and knowledge and providing examples of activities and children's work
- Outlining the school's policy on equal opportunities in relation to IT and alerting parents to the inhibiting effects of gender stereotyping

The relationship between the school and the home is probably at its strongest at the infant stage. Directing parents' anxieties, enthusiasm and energies to the good of the child helps minimise any conflicts between home and school and reinforces the learning which is taking place.

Summary

In this final chapter, we have examined the production and development of a school policy for IT. It has been suggested that the process of producing a policy statement is often more valuable than the end result.

The issue of equal opportunities and the unique nature of IT has been explored and the creation, evolution and review of the school's scheme of work is examined in relation to the progressive and continuous development of children's IT capability.

Aspects of in-service education for IT are examined, with an emphasis on approaches to effective school-based INSET and guidance for those preparing for an OFSTED inspection.

It should be borne in mind that up until about 15 years ago none of us had seen, let alone laid hands on, a desktop computer, and 13 years is the school lifetime of one child. For a subject which is barely out of school itself, IT has come a long way. It still has a lot to learn but gets more manageable, biddable and easier to understand as it grows. Just like a child! For ...

> "To err is human, but to really foul things up requires a computer!" (Anon.)

References

Hargreaves, A. (1989) *Curriculum and Assessment Reform*; Open University Press

Impact (1994) *Information Technology in Schools: The Impact of the IT in Schools Initiative*, 1990–1993; HMSO

Martin, R. (1991) School Children's Attitudes towards Computers as a Function of Gender, Course Subjects and the Availability of Home Computers; *Journal of Computer Assisted Learning*, vol. 7 (3), pp. 189–94

OFSTED (1995) *Information Technology: A Review of Inspection Findings, 1993/4;* HMSO

Appendix I: Glossary of educational IT terminology

Terms that appear in italic are defined in their appropriate alphabetical place in the glossary.

adventure program	A *program* which usually puts the user in an imaginary situation. The user is required to take decisions to control the way the adventure progresses. The most well known educational adventure program is *Granny's Garden* (4mation).
airbrush	In a *graphics program*, a tool which simulates the effect of an airbrush or spray can
application	A computer *program* which is specifically designed for one kind of activity (e.g. a *word processor* is an application which handles text)
bug	An error in a computer *program* which may cause the computer to "crash"
byte	A unit of memory measurement comprising 8 bits. Each letter displayed on a computer screen occupies one byte of computer memory. 1000 bytes = 1 kilobyte (k), 1000 k = 1 megabyte (Mb), 1000 Mb = 1 gigabyte (Gb)
CAD	Computer Aided (or Assisted) Design
CBL	Computer Based Learning
CD ROM drive	A form of *disk drive* which stores information on optical disks. A *ROM* drive is used for extracting information from the disk but cannot be used for writing or storing information created by the user.
clip file	A *file* of items specifically prepared for inclusion in other files. Clip-art files contain graphic images, clip-sound files contain sounds, and so on.
concept keyboard	An *input device* comprising a tablet (A4- or A3-sized) connected to the computer on which overlays can be placed. By pressing different areas of the tablet, actions can be made to happen on the computer (sounds; letters, words, phrases of text; pictures; animations; the control of *output devices* such as a *turtle* robot).
content-free software	Higher level programs which permit more control of the computer by the user. A *word processor* is content free.
control	The means by which the action of a device is directed. A computer can be made to control a device to which it is connected, such as a *disk drive*, a printer, a model or robot.
copy	An editing term: the duplication of an item (text, image, sound) to be subsequently *pasted* elsewhere in the same document or transferred to another *file*

cursor	The flashing mark which appears on the screen to show where text will appear when a key is pressed on the *keyboard*. A cursor's shape can be changed. Depending on its shape, a cursor is also called an I bar, a caret, an insertion point, a mouse pointer, a tool, etc.
cut	An editing term: to remove an item (text, image, sound) which can subsequently be *pasted* elsewhere in the same file or transferred to another *file*
data logging	A means by which a computer monitors an environmental event and stores *data* arising from this event. For example, a computer can be set up to sample the temperature in a room at 10-minute intervals and store the data over a period of a week.
data	The "raw" information which a computer handles. Data can take the form of text, numbers or pictures.
database	A computer *application* enabling information to be stored, retrieved and manipulated. The most common form of database is the "flat file" which resembles a card index system in structure.
desktop publishing	An *application* for designing and producing documents that may include text, headings and illustrations
dialogue box	A *window* which appears on screen giving information which requires a response
digital camera	A camera which "takes" an image and stores it as an electronic signal which can be *downloaded* directly into a computer
digitiser	A piece of *software* which transforms a video signal into a digital signal which can be manipulated by the computer
dip switch	A small switch (usually in a bank of 8 or more) usually found in a *printer*. Setting the dip switches to different positions controls the way the printer behaves.
directory	A collection of *files* is stored in a directory. A directory is usually given a name to help identify the files it contains.
disk drive	A device used for storing computer information on magnetic or optical disks. Schools make use of *floppy, hard* and optical (*CD ROM*) *disk drives*.
download	The term describing the transfer of information from one computer to another (such as through a *modem*)
drill and practice	Low-level educational programs which are designed to provide instruction or practice with specific skills (e.g. spelling, addition)
e-mail	A means of sending messages between two computers connected via a *network*
error message	A message which the computer sends to communicate to the user that there is a problem

export	To transfer information from one *application* to another
file	Information that is stored, usually on a *disk drive*. A file is given a name to help identify it.
firmware	The *programs* which are built into a computer such as those used to *control* the way the screen appears
floppy disk	A form of *disk* used for storing information in electronic form. The plastic case contains a disk of magnetic material, similar to that used in audio and video recorders. Floppy disks store a maximum of 1.6 *kilobytes* of information.
function key	A key (usually labelled F0, F1, F2, etc.) which is used by an *application* to perform a particular task (e.g. *printing* or *saving* a document)
gigabyte	See *byte*
graphics program	An *application* which enables the user to create or manipulate images on screen
hard disk	Most modern computers have internal hard disk drives. Similar to a *floppy disk*, a hard disk is capable of holding larger amounts of information.
hardware	Computer devices such as the *printer*, the *monitor*, the keyboard and *mouse*
highlight	To marking an area of the screen, usually for editing. Most *applications* show highlighted areas in reverse colours (e.g. white on black rather than black on white).
icon	A small graphic image (or picture) which can be selected with the *mouse pointer*. Most applications have an icon which represents them on the screen.
import	See *export*
information technology	Electronic means by which information is stored, manipulated and transmitted
input device	A piece of *hardware* for entering information into a computer. A keyboard is an input device for entering text into the computer
interface	A device for connecting equipment to a computer. A *modem* is a form of interface, as it connects the computer to a telephone line.
Internet	A global *network* linking computers
joystick	An *input device* which allows control of objects or images on the screen through the movement of a lever, most often used for computer "arcade" games

justification
The manipulation of text on a line in a *word processor*. "Right justify" aligns all lines to end against the right margin, "Left justify" aligns the beginning of lines to the left of the screen and "Fully justified" inserts additional gaps between words to begin and end in line with both margins.

kilobyte (k)
See *byte*

laptop computer
See *portable computer*

LCD screen
Liquid Crystal Display screen: a thin form of monitor screen (about the thickness of two pieces of glass). Electrical charges cause different areas of the screen to change colour.

load
To transfer information from a storage device (such as a *disk drive*) into the computer's memory

LOGO
A computer programming language whereby instructions are written to control the actions of the computer. LOGO was written by Seymour Papert (among others) to provide a "low floor, high ceiling" approach to programming – easy enough for infants to use, potentially complex enough to challenge graduates

megabyte (Mb)
See *byte*

menu
A list of options which can be selected by use of a *mouse pointer*

menu bar
A section of the screen (across the top with PC and Macintosh computers, across the bottom of the screen with Acorn computers) on which *menus* or the *icons* of *applications* are placed

merge
To bring two different pieces of information together in the same document or *file*. For example, picture files can be merged with text in some *word processors*.

MIDI
Musical Instrument Digital Interface – a system (set of agreed guidelines to ensure conformity) for connecting musical instruments to computers

model
A representation of a situation which enables predictions to be made. Mathematics is used to model reality (e.g. when three objects are placed with four objects, there will be seven objects all together). A computer uses mathematical algorithms to model quite complex situations (e.g. global weather patterns).

modem
An electronic device which connects a computer to a telephone line enabling information to be transferred between computers. A modem is required for connection to the *Internet*. Fax modems enable faxes to be sent and received.

monitor
An *output device*: the screen by which the computer communicates with the user

mouse	A computer *input device*: a small plastic box which rests on the table beside a computer. By moving the mouse and pressing one, two or three buttons, images can be made to move on the computer screen or actions made to happen.
mouse pointer	See *cursor*
multimedia	An *application* which makes use of text, *graphics* and sound
network	A system whereby computers are interlinked. A local network links computers on the same site (e.g. within a school). The *Internet* is a global network.
operating system	The internal *software* which controls the way a computer operates. "Windows 95" is a PC operating system.
output device	A piece of *hardware* which enables the computer to communicate with the outside world. A *printer* is an output device.
palmtop computer	See *portable computer*
paste	An editing term: to place a previously *cut* item in a *file* or document
peripheral	A piece of computer equipment which is not situated within the computer. Most *printers* are peripheral devices; they are separately plugged into the computer.
photo CD	A CD ROM on which photographic images are stored. An ordinary colour print film can be processed by most high street chemists into a photo CD (for a small extra charge) enabling photographic images to be *imported* directly into the computer
pirate software	*Software* which has been copied illegally. Good software takes considerable time and effort to write, illegal copying denies the writers their income which will ultimately lead to poorer quality or excessively priced software
pocket computer	See *portable computer*
podule	An electronic circuit board which is plugged inside a computer to extend its capabilities
pointer	See *cursor*
port	A socket on a computer
portable computer	A small computer. A laptop computer is about the size of a small attaché case. A palmtop or pocket computer is about the size of an adult's hand.
posterisation	A graphics effect which changes an image to resemble a posterised photograph. A posterised image exaggerates contrasts (e.g. reduces an image to stark black and white).

printer	An *output device* for producing paper-based copies. Three main types of printer are used in schools – dot matrix, inkjet and laserjet. Dot matrix printers are cheap but are noisy and produce a poor image; inkjets are relatively cheap, but use water-based inks; laser jets provide high quality images but are more expensive
program	A list of instructions to control the operation of a computer; the term is also used as a verb, meaning to provide such as a list.
programmable turtle	A device which children can program to move by carrying out a series of instructions
programming language	A particular vocabulary of instructions which can be used to control a computer
pull-down menu	See *menu*
RAM	Random Access Memory: part of a computer's memory which is used for storing *loaded programs* and *files*
ROM	Read Only Memory: part of the computer's memory which contains fixed information such as the computer's *operating system* and other *firmware*
save	To transfer information from the computer's memory to a storage device such as a *disk drive*.
scanner	A flatbed scanner looks like a photocopier; it transforms paper-based information into digital information so that it can be used by a computer. A hand-held scanner is a smaller device which performs the same function but it is "swiped" across a piece of paper-based information.
sensor	A device that a computer can use to monitor external events such as temperature or light levels
shareware	*Software* which does not have to be paid for until it is used. Shareware can be *downloaded* from the *Internet*.
simulation	A computer *model* of a situation: the user can enter information into the simulation and the computer will respond with an appropriate outcome. Simulations make it possible to model expensive, difficult, complex, hazardous or impossible situations.
software	The *programs* (or procedures) used to instruct the computer
sort	To put items into order (alphabetical or numerical). This process is often used by *databases* and *spreadsheets*. Some word processors allow paragraphs to be sorted.
speech	See *voice synthesis*
spreadsheet	A computer *application* which resembles a large grid of cells. Each cell can be linked to any other by a formula. If information is changed in one cell, all other interlinked cells are changed according to the linking formulae.

system software	See *operating system*
tiling	A means of graphical manipulation whereby a "tile" is created and tessellated with itself using reflections and rotations on screen
trackerball	An *input* device which controls the *mouse pointer* by means of a large ball mounted in a cradle – similar in action to an upturned *mouse*
turtle	See *programmable turtle*
upload	To send information to another computer
user group	A group of like-minded people who have a similar interest. User groups communicate over the *Internet*.
VDU	Visual Display Unit – see *monitor*
VGA	Video Graphics Array – a standard which specifies the way computers communicate with *monitors* to ensure conformity
virus	A computer virus is a rogue *program* which "infects" a computer's *operating system,* usually through its *hard disk*. Viruses upset the normal working of a computer (i.e. changing files to gibberish). Some viruses can damage a computer by, for example, making the *hard drive* rattle itself to pieces. Viruses are often transferred from one computer to another by *floppy disks* or over the *Internet*. All hard-drive-based machines should have virus protection *software* installed.
voice synthesis	A software *application* which simulates the sound of the human voice, usually comprising a series of phonemes (phonetic sounds) which are constructed by the computer to form words
WIMP	*Windows, Icons, Menus, Pointers* – the devices that are used to operate most *mouse*-based computers
window	A framed area of the computer screen. Several windows can be displayed on the screen. Usually only one window is "active" at any one time and is able to be used.
word processor	An *application* for manipulating text
World Wide Web	Part of the *Internet* which communicates information in text, images, sounds and animation using "hypertext". By moving the *mouse pointer* over parts of a World Wide Web page and clicking a *mouse* button , the user is given more information or is transferred to other web "sites".
zoom	To magnify part of an image for more detailed work, or to reduce the size of an image to see more of it on screen

Appendix II: Guidance on hardware

(See Chapter 2 for more generalised information.)

All educational hardware suppliers now market hard-disk-based, multimedia computers which include built-in CD ROM drives. When purchasing hardware, the following questions may prove useful when speaking to suppliers:

- Does the price include the monitor?
- What size and resolution is the monitor? (A recommended standard would be a 14-inch VGA monitor with a dot pitch of 0.28mm or, if finances allow, a super VGA MultiSynch, with a 17inch screen,)
- Does the price include the keyboard?
- What software is included with the computer?
- Does it include a filing system designed for use by young children?
- Is there any warranty period – what kind of support is available (technical and/or educational)?

IBM PC-compatible computers

Most PC computers are IBM-compatible, these days and you tend to get what you pay for (from £800 to you name it!). In a survey of PCs carried out by *PC Magazine* (August, 1996), the following manufacturers came out as producing the most reliable computers (in order of most reliable):

1. Hewlett Packard
2. Research Machines
3. Apple Macintosh
4. Viglen
5. Digital
6. Dan
7. Gateway
8. Dell
9. IBM
10. Compaq

Research Machines (RM)

Research Machines have for a long time supported primary education in this country. Their PC-compatible computers are quite competitively priced and can be purchased with a bundle of software and a specially designed filing system for use with Key Stage 1 children (*Infant Window Box*). Their educational support, software production and training programmes are comprehensive and founded on experience. For those considering a change to PC computers, RM are worth considering.

Xemplar (Apple Macintosh/Acorn)

The education wings of both Apple Macintosh and Acorn computers have joined forces recently to provide a combined educational support service. Apple Macintosh computers have a very easy to use (intuitive) operating system on which all other Windows and mouse-driven systems have been based. Acorn computers (who used to manufacture the BBC B computer) have a long tradition of educational support in the UK. Xemplar has produced an easy-to-use filing system designed for use by primary children (*Junior Toolbox*) which includes a set of programs specially selected to address all areas of the National Curriculum. Although the system looks identical on both Apple and Acorn computers, disks and software cannot be easily exchanged between the two types of machine.

Peripherals

Printers

Dot matrix printers can still be purchased. They are the ones which make a lot of noise and use a ribbon like a typewriter's. Dot matrix printers tend to be the cheapest (£50–£150), as are their ink ribbons. Some print in colour but the quality of print is not high.

Ink-jet printers are now the most common type. They are relatively cheap (£100–£300). They produce good quality images in black and white or colour, but the ink is water-based and will smudge if the page gets wet. The ink cartridges (especially colour) can be quite expensive.

Laser-jet printers are the most expensive (£250–£1000) but produce the best quality images. Laser-jet cartridges can be very expensive but last considerably longer than ink-jet cartridges. The image produced does not fade and is water resistant.

Keyboards

The concept keyboard has been in production for many years and is very reliable. The keyboard can be used by most computers but to get the correct lead you must specify which type of computer will be used. A number of educational programs for young children include a concept keyboard option, but check first as it will not work with them all. The keyboards are available in A4 and A3 sizes at about £120.

For other types of keyboard and input devices for children with physical difficulties, refer to the catalogues of SEMERC (Tel. 0161-627 4469, e-mail info@semerc.demon.co.uk) or Don Jonston (Tel. 01925-241642).

Appendix III: Suggested software

(See Chapter 2 for more generalised information.)

	BBC B	Acorn Archimedes	RM / PC	Apple
Simple word talking processor	*Stylus* (MAPE)	*Talking Textease* (Softease) *Pages* (SEMERC) *Talkwrite* (Resource)	*Talking Textease* (Softease) *Pages* (SEMERC) *Talking Word for Windows* (Longman Logotron)	*Write Out Loud* (Don Johnston)
Powerful word processor	*Pendown* (Longman Logotron)	*Pendown* (Longman Logotron)	*Word for Windows* (Microsoft)	*Word 6.0* (Microsoft)
Simple graphics program	*Paintpot 2* (Kids' Academy) *Ollie Octopus Sketch Pad* (Storm)	*Splosh* (Kudlian) *Doodle* (SEMERC)	*Tiny Draw Plus* (Topologika) *Splat!* (Spa) *First Paint* (Resource)	*Claris Works* (Claris) with *EasyWorks* (Claris)
Sophisticated graphics program		*Kidpix 2* (ESM) *Dazzle* (SEMERC) *Revelation 2* (Longman Logotron)	*Kidpix 2* (Broderbund) *Paintspa Plus* (Spa) *Flying Colours* (Ablac) *Dazzle* (SEMERC) *Claris Draw* (Claris)	*Kidpix 2* (Broderbund) *Flying Colours* (Ablac) *Claris Draw* (Claris)
Clip files	*Picture Packs* (Resource)	*Picture Packs* (Resource) *Just Pictures* (SEMERC) *Just Sounds* (SEMERC) *Graphics Explosion Deluxe* (Ablac)	*Picture Packs* (Resource) *Key Photo Gallery* (Softkey) *Just Pictures* (SEMERC) *Just Sounds* (SEMERC) *Graphics Explosion Deluxe* (Ablac)	*Picture Packs* (Resource) *Key Photo Gallery* (Softkey) *Just Pictures* (SEMERC) *Just Sounds* (SEMERC) *Graphics Explosion Deluxe* (Ablac)
Simple music program	*Compose* (ESP)	*Music Box* (Topologika) *Music Maker* (Resource) *Compose World* (ESP) *Beetles* (SEMERC)	*Music Box* (Topologika) *Music Maker* (Resource)	
Desktop publishing package	*Fairy Tales* (Resource)	*Junior DTP* (Eric) *Bookmaker* (Resource) *Pages* (SEMERC)	*Pages* (SEMERC) *Bookmaker 1* (Resource) *Easybook* (Sunburst)	*Easybook* (Sunburst)
Multimedia authoring		*Hyperstudio* (TAG) *Ultima* (SEMERC)	*Hyperstudio* (TAG)	*Hyperstudio* (TAG) *Storybook Weaver* (TAG) *Imagination Express* (Iona)
Simple database	*All about Me* (Northern Micromedia) *Our Facts* (supplied free with first Computers for Schools project)	*Dataframe* (Resource) *All about Me* (Northern Micromedia) *1st Find It!* (Appian Way) *Picturepoint* (Longman Logotron)	*All about Me* (Northern Micromedia) *1st Find It!* (Appian Way) *Base One for Windows* (SEMERC)	*Claris Works* (Claris) with *EasyWorks* (Claris)
More powerful database	*Key* (Anglia TV)	*Find It!* (Appian Way) *Junior Pinpoint* (Longman Logotron)	*Find It!* (Appian Way) *Junior Pinpoint* (Longman Logotron)	*Claris Works* (Claris)

Simple spreadsheet	*Cambridge Spreadsheet* (Cambridgeshire Software House) *Pigeonhole* (Northern Micromedia)	*Junior Spreadsheet* (ERIC) *Sheetwise!* (SEMERC) *Keycount* (Anglia TV) *Cambridge Spreadsheet* (Cambridgeshire Software House)	*Cambridge Spreadsheet* (Cambridgeshire Software House) *Sparks!* (Spa) *Pigeonhole* (Northern Micromedia)	*Claris Works* (Claris) with *EasyWorks* (Claris)
Graph-drawing program	*Graph IT!* (MAPE)	*Graphplot* (SEMERC)	*Graphplot* (SEMERC) *Counter for Windows* (Black Cat)	
Suite of programs			*Claris Works* (Claris) *Claris Primary Templates* (Claris) *EasyWorks* (Claris)	Claris Works (Claris) *Claris Primary Templates* (Claris) *EasyWorks* (Claris)
General adventure program	*Albert's House* (Resource) *Granny's Garden* (4mation) *Dreamtime* (Sherston)	*Albert's House* (Resource) *Granny's Garden* (4mation) *Dreamtime* (Sherston)	*Albert's House* (Resource) *Granny's Garden* (4mation) *Silly Noisy House* (Voyager)	*Albert's House* (Resource) *Silly Noisy House* (Voyager)
Programmable turtle robot	*Roamer* (Valiant) *Pip* (Swallow)	*Roamer* (Valiant) *Pip* (Swallow)	*Roamer* (Valiant) *Pip* (Swallow)	*Roamer* (Valiant) *Pip* (Swallow)
Simulation or adventure which requires children to sequence events		*The Playground* (Topologika) *Crystal Rainforest* (Sherston)	*Crystal Rainforest* (Sherston)	*Crystal Rainforest* (Sherston)
Introductory version of LOGO		*First LOGO* (Longman Logotron) *Tiny LOGO* (Topologika)	*First LOGO* (Longman Logotron) *Tiny LOGO* (Topologika)	*Microworlds* (LCSI)
Full version of LOGO	*BBC LOGO* (Longman Logotron)	*WinLogo* (Longman Logotron)	*WinLogo* (Longman Logotron)	*Apple LOGO*
Floppy-disk-based talking books		*Cambridge Reading* (Sherston) *Look Here! Talking Topics* (Sherston) *Oxford Reading Tree* (Sherston)	*Cambridge Reading* (Sherston) *Look Here! Talking Topics* (Sherston) *Oxford Reading Tree* (Sherston)	*Cambridge Reading* (Sherston *Look Here! Talking Topics* (Sherston) *Oxford Reading Tree* (Sherston)
CD ROM based talking books		*Talking Stories* (Broderbund) *Little Red Riding Hood* etc. (Tempest Publishing)	*Talking Stories* (Broderbund) *Little Red Riding Hood* etc. (Tempest Publishing) *Topsy and Tim series* (Longman Logotron) *Beatrix Potter stories* (Mindscape)	*Talking Stories* (Broderbund) *Beatrix Potter stories* (Mindscape)
CD ROM reference		*Children's Micropaedia 96* (Kingfisher)	*Children's Micropaedia 96* (Kingfisher) *Explorapaedia* (Microsoft) *My First Incredible Dictionary* (Dorling Kindersley)	*My First Incredible Dictionary* (Dorling Kindersley)

Note: Software can be purchased directly from the companies listed above or from generalist suppliers such as: AVP (Tel. 01291-625439), REM (Tel. 01458-253636), TAG (Tel. 0800-591262), SCET (Tel. 0800-591262).

Appendix IV: The National Curriculum and IT at Key Stage 1 *(1995 orders)*

General requirements

Information Technology (IT) is characterised by an ability to use IT tools and information sources effectively to analyse, process and present information, and to model, measure and control external events. This involves:

- using information sources and IT tools to solve problems;
- using IT tools and information sources such as computer systems and software packages, to support learning in a variety of contexts;
- understanding the implications of IT for working life and society.

Pupils should be given opportunities, where appropriate, to develop and apply their IT capability in their study of National Curriculum subjects.

Key Stage 1 Programme of Study for IT

Pupils should be taught to use IT equipment and software confidently and purposefully to communicate and handle information, and to support their problem solving, recording and expressive work.

1 *Pupils should be given opportunities to:*

   a use a variety of equipment and software, including microcomputers and various keyboards, to carry out a variety of functions in a range of contexts;

   b explore the use of computer systems and control technology in everyday life;

   c examine and discuss their experience of IT and look at the use of IT in the outside world.

2 *Communicating and handling information*

   Pupils should be taught to:

   a generate and communicate their ideas in different forms, using text, tables, pictures and sound;

   b enter and store information;

   c retrieve, process and display information that has been stored.

3 *Controlling and modelling*

   Pupils should be taught to:

   a recognise that control is integral to many everyday devices;

   b give direct signals or commands that produce a variety of outcomes, and describe the effects of their actions;

   c use IT-based models or simulations to explore aspects of real and imaginary situations.

Level descriptions

By the end of Key Stage 1 the performance of the majority of pupils should be within the range of Levels 1 to 3.

- *Level 1*

  Pupils use IT to assemble text and symbols to help them communicate ideas. They explore information held on IT systems, showing an awareness that information exists in a variety of forms. They recognise that many everyday devices respond to signals and commands, and that they can select options when using such devices to produce different outcomes.

- *Level 2*

  Pupils use IT to help them generate and communicate ideas in different forms, such as text, tables, pictures and sound. With some support, they retrieve and store work. They use IT to sort and classify information and to present their findings. Pupils control devices purposefully and describe the effects of their actions. They use IT-based models or simulations to investigate options as they explore aspects of real and imaginary situations.

- *Level 3*

  Pupils use IT to generate, amend, organise and present ideas. They use IT to save data and to access stored information, following straightforward lines of enquiry. They understand how to control equipment to achieve specific outcomes by giving a series of instructions. They use IT-based models or simulations to help them make decisions, and are aware of the consequences of their choices. They describe their use of IT, and its use in the outside world.

Specific references to the use of IT in the programmes of study in other National Curriculum Key Stage 1 Programmes of Study

All subjects (apart from PE) include the following requirement:

Pupils should be given opportunities, where appropriate, to develop and apply their information technology (IT) capability in their study of [the subject].

English

Reading – Range

b Pupils should be introduced to and should read information, both in print form and on screen. They should be encouraged to make use of a range of sources of information, including dictionaries, IT-based reference materials, encyclopaedias and information presented in fictional form.

Writing – Key Skills

b Pupils should have opportunities to plan and review their writing, assembling and developing their ideas on paper and on screen.

Mathematics

Using and Applying Mathematics

4 Developing mathematical reasoning

b ask questions including "What would happen if?" and "Why?" e.g. considering the behaviour of a programmable toy;

Number

1 Pupils should be given opportunities to:

d use calculators both as a means to explore number and as a tool for calculating with realistic data, e.g. numbers with several digits;

f use computer software, including a database.

2 Developing an understanding of place value

c recognise and use in context simple fractions, including halves and quarters, decimal notation in recording money, and negative numbers, e.g. a temperature scale, a number line, a calculator display.

3 Understanding relationships between numbers and developing methods of computation

e use a basic calculator, reading the display, e.g. use the constant function to explore repeated addition.

4 Solving numerical problems

c choose a suitable method of computation, using apparatus where appropriate, or a calculator where the number has several digits.

Shape, Space and Measures

1 Pupils should be given opportunities to:

b use IT devices, e.g. programmable toys, turtle graphics packages.

3 Understanding and using properties of position and movement

b understand angle as a measure of turn and recognise quarter turns, e.g. giving instructions for rotating a programmable toy; recognise right angles.

Science

1 Systematic enquiry

d use IT to collect, store, retrieve and present scientific information.

History

3 Interpretations of history

a Pupils should be taught to identify different ways in which the past is represented, e.g. pictures, written accounts, films, television programmes, plays, songs, reproductions of objects, museum displays.

Geography

Geographical skills

3 Pupils should be taught to:

f use secondary sources, e.g. pictures, photographs (including aerial photographs), books, videos, CD ROM encyclopaedia, to obtain information.

Music

1 Pupils should be given opportunities to:

b make appropriate use of IT to record sounds.

Note: All statements in normal text are statutory requirements, examples in italic are non-statutory.

It is important to appreciate that *all* school subject planning documentation (apart from PE) should include references to the contribution made by the subject to the development of children's IT capability. This is to address the "catch-all" requirement included in the introduction to National Curriculum documentation for each subject.

Index